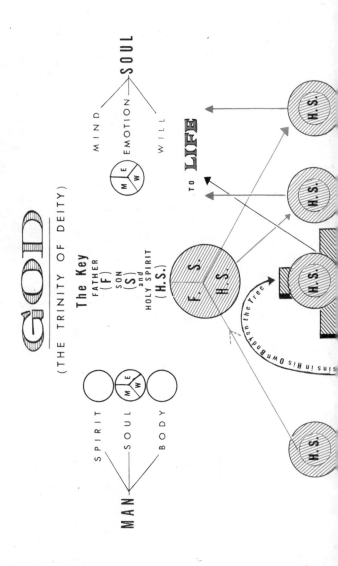

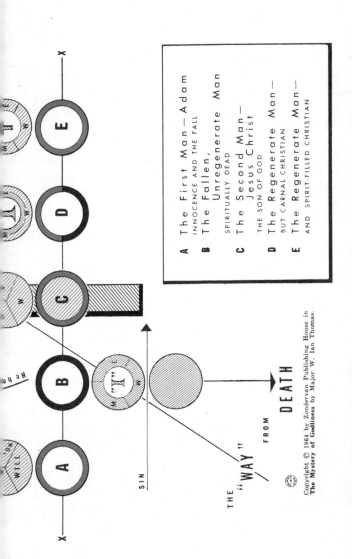

A The First Man — Adam
   INNOCENCE AND THE FALL

B The Fallen,
   Unregenerate Man
   SPIRITUALLY DEAD

C The Second Man —
   Jesus Christ
   THE SON OF GOD

D The Regenerate Man —
   BUT CARNAL CHRISTIAN

E The Regenerate Man —
   AND SPIRIT-FILLED CHRISTIAN

THE "WAY"   FROM

DEATH

SIN

Copyright © 1964 by Zondervan Publishing House in
The Mystery of Godliness by Major W. Ian Thomas.

The Mystery of Godliness

The
Mystery of Godliness

by
MAJOR W. IAN THOMAS

ZONDERVAN
PUBLISHING HOUSE
OF THE ZONDERVAN CORPORATION | GRAND RAPIDS, MICHIGAN 49506

Library of Congress Catalog Card Number 64-11948

Seventh printing (Zondervan
  Books edition) November 1971
Seventeenth printing 1981
ISBN 0-310-33252-4

Printed in the United States of America

Dedicated to my wife,
JOAN,
and to my three sons,
CHRISTOPHER,
MARK,
and
PETER
*for being such a wonderful
team in such a wonderful Saviour.*

CONTENTS

1

THE QUALITY OF TRUE COMMITMENT

But Jesus did not commit himself unto them, because he knew all men (John 2:24).

All that glitters is not gold, and in the light of all that we are about to consider, it may well be profitable for us to make a sober re-evaluation of those standards of commitment which are prevalent today, and which pass muster for Christian dedication.

All too often quantity takes precedence over quality, and in this highly competitive age those outward appearances of "success" which are calculated to enhance the reputation of the professional preacher, or the prestige of those who have promoted him, are of greater importance than the abiding consequences of his ministry.

In an unholy ambition to get "results," the end too often justifies the means, with the result that the *means* are certainly not always beyond suspicion, and the "results," to say the least, extremely dubious!

In this unhappy situation both the pulpit and the pew carry their share of the blame, though I suspect that it started in the pulpit! There are those who have insisted that to be valid, every spiritual transaction between the believer and his Lord must be matched by some outward physical act, and that apart from the accompanying act, no worth can be attached to the inward spiritual transaction.

Inevitably on the basis of this unfounded supposition, the work of the Holy Spirit in any given meeting through the ministry of the preacher, will be directly represented by the physical response of the congrega-

9

tion to some form of public appeal, "invitation" or so-called "altar-call"—a term which is singularly inappropriate in view of the fact that the Lord Jesus Christ has "offered one sacrifice for sins forever" (Hebrews 10:12), and there is no place today for another sacrifice or for another altar in the church of the redeemed—the *altar* has given place to a *throne* for the exalted Lamb!

The terrible dangers inherent in such a fallacy, however, are patently obvious!

The ambitious preacher, eager to climb the ladder of evangelical fame, and not altogether unmoved by the plight of the lost and the needs of the saints, will be subject to a temptation so strong, that for more than one it has proved to be irresistible—that of being heavily preoccupied with devising ways and means of ensuring that a large enough public "response" on the part of the congregation will adequately demonstrate the effectiveness of his preaching, vindicate his reputation, sufficiently reward the confidence of his sponsors, and suitably impress the crowd.

The preacher, of course, will not allow himself to be aware of the underlying motives which prompt the use of his clever techniques, being careful to persuade himself that they stem only from what he would describe as a genuine "passion for souls," but the sorry spectacle is exposed for what it is by the apparent indifference on the part of the preacher to the tragic aftermath of his endeavors, once "the show is over"!

It is little wonder that the "pulpit," having drilled the "pew" into submission, now finds itself the victim of its own ill-conceived imposition, for the community which has been taught to accept outward, physical response to some public "invitation" as the criterion of spiritual success on the part of the preacher, invariably demands this tangible evidence of success on every occasion in which he engages in his ministry.

Thus the pastor of a small church, trapped in the grip of this vicious circle, may succeed over a period of

10

time in bringing the whole of his congregation "out to the front"—to stand at the communion rail in response to his many appeals—but having had all his people out once, it will be incumbent upon him to get them out all over again, and again, and yet *again* if his fervor and his zeal are not to be called into question by his church officers, and his pastorate, maybe, become vacant!

The pastor has no option under such circumstances, but to whittle down the commitment he demands until its whole value and meaning has been lost, for it can never be final, otherwise he would preach himself out of business! Instead of being faced with complete capitulation to the Lord Jesus Christ, and final, irrevocable abandonment to all His will, the believer is presented again and again with "baby" issues, all of which should be comprehended in the greater, basic issue of true discipleship!

It is much easier to confront a person with his *sins* than it is to confront him with his "sin," for as will be fully demonstrated in later chapters of this book, "sin" is an attitude which affects a man's fundamental relationship to God; it has to do with what a man *is*; whereas "sins" have to do with what a man *does,* and we all have a happy knack of being able to detach what we *do* from what we *are*! We are all highly skilled in the art of self-justification and are able to produce innumerable reasons as to why what we did was excusable—even if it was wrong! We can even feel heroic, and almost virtuous, in accepting the blame for that which so obviously (*to us!*) was only the *natural*, almost inevitable reaction to enticing, compelling or provocative circumstances or people! For this reason a man can admit and be sorry for what he has done, without admitting that what he has done is a result of what he is.

On this basis a person may be called upon a hundred times to face the lesser issues of what he has done, without once being confronted with the greater issue of

11

what he is—indeed the "comfort" to be found in confession, bringing freedom from fear, and relief to a bad conscience will eliminate for him the need for any basic change in his fundamental relationship to God. This kind of confession falls hopelessly short of real repentance, and remains unmatched by any change of purpose; Moses reduced his people to tears again and again—but it left them in the wilderness! They still had no heart for Canaan! There was no lack of response to Moses' preaching, but they would not do business with God! "And they said unto Moses, Speak thou with us, and we will hear: but let not God speak with us, lest we die" (Exodus 20:19).

They wanted second-hand religion! They wanted neither godlessness nor godliness—they did not know how to live, and were afraid to die! Commitment to them was on the installment system, and Moses was their broker!

Second-hand religion may keep a preacher in business, and make him indispensable to his congregation, but it cannot produce discipleship; there will be no spontaneity of action, nor any other evidence of that divine initiative in man which springs only from man's total availability to God.

True commitment to the Lord Jesus Christ gives Him "right of way," and releases His Life through you in all the freshness and power of divine action, so that according to His gracious promise, out of your innermost being "springs and rivers of living water may flow continuously" (John 7:38, *Amplified New Testament*) —and you do not have to push a river! It cuts its own channel, and cleanses as it flows!

In drawing attention to those glaring abuses which have done so much to discredit modern evangelism and convention ministry, I do not suggest for one moment, that there is not a legitimate place for the public confession of faith in Christ, nor would I insist that true commitment to Christ may never be accompanied by an outward witness to the fact. That would be to throw away the baby with the bath-water, for without a doubt, there are many who have been greatly helped in their decision *for* Christ, or in their commitment *to* Christ by a wise, gracious invitation to *act,* rather than further to delay in yielding obedience to the Truth.

My plea is simply for *reality*—on God's terms of reference! It is for this reason also, that no matter how intensely I may dislike the shallowness and showmanship of many, in their abuse of the holy art of preaching by the use of doubtful "response techniques," I cannot on the other hand, endorse in any way the empty accusation made by the champions of hollow, ritualistic formalism, that all activity outside the established "practice of religion" within the "respectable church systems" is of necessity all "mere ignorant emotionalism." That is sheer nonsense!

If there remains much to be desired in the quality of commitment prevalent today in evangelical circles, and in the world-wide evangelistic out-reach of that great body of born-again believers which is the true church of Jesus Christ in all denominations—even more to be deplored are those wholesale opportunities for practicing hypocrisy provided by those formal, public acts of commitment to Christ common to so many of the denominations, which in the vast majority of cases are totally devoid of any spiritual content, and which serve only to satisfy the traditional "niceties" of religious observance in an otherwise godless society!

Whether it be by baptism as an infant or as an adult, by "sprinkling" or by "immersion"; whether it be by confirmation in the early "teens," or by any other public act of dedication and acceptance into full church membership, there must be very few in the "Christianized" countries of Western Europe who have not in one way or another, "committed themselves to Christ"— yet by what strange twist of the mind or willful stretch of the imagination, any ecclesiastical hierarchy of any

13

given church system can credit this performance with any real spiritual validity, when over 90% of the populations of these countries never darken a church door to worship God, is beyond all intelligent explanation!

The Lord Jesus Christ is neither accepted as Saviour, nor honored and obeyed as Lord, yet the rubber-stamp of church approval has been granted, and is considered by the overwhelming majority to be an altogether adequate discharge of their responsibility toward God, and a formidable defence against the unwelcome attentions of those who would insist upon a reality of spiritual experience, which has neither been demanded nor expected by their "church!"

If church attendance in the United States, representing something like 60% of the population, far and away exceeds that of any other Protestant country at this time, it should be a matter for genuine thankfulness to God—yet there are few countries in the world where there are so many crimes of violence, so much juvenile delinquency, so much drug addiction and so many alcoholics, and where there is such widespread graft and corruption in government and commerce. Are only *those* responsible for this sorry record who have never conformed to the requirements of the church, in some outward, formal act of dedication?

Why should international world Communism with its fanatical convictions, its thorough indoctrination and utter dedication, be afraid of this flabby monster called "the church," with its countless millions of nominal adherents who know neither conviction nor concern—who are colorless, spiritual non-entities, knowing neither what they believe, nor believing what they know! Utterly without any sense of mission, and governed by and large by men who are themselves riddled through and through with infidelity, boastful of their own wanton repudiation of all the essential ingredients of the faith they profess to proclaim! A Christendom whose worst enemies are within its own ranks!

14

The Word of God to the Jews in Paul's day, might well be the Word of God to Christendom today:

> For, as it is written, The name of God is maligned *and* blasphemed among the Gentiles because of you! — The words to this effect are from [your own] Scriptures . . . For he is not a [real] Jew who is only one outwardly *and* publicly, nor is [true] circumcision something external and physical. But he is a Jew who is one inwardly, and [true] circumcision is of the heart, a spiritual and not a literal [matter]. His praise is not from men but from God (Romans 2:24, 28, 29, *Amplified New Testament*).

It was into just such a situation that the Lord Jesus Christ entered, as at the Feast of the Passover He received such a tumultuous welcome in Jerusalem. "Hosanna to the son of David!" they cried. "Blessed be he that cometh in the name of the Lord: Hosanna in the highest" (Matthew 21:9).

No doubt the disciples were flushed with excitement and highly delighted that their Master should receive such a tremendous ovation—yet maybe there were some among them who had their misgivings! If only He could be prevailed upon not to say the wrong thing! If only they could persuade Him *just this once,* not to do anything which would spoil it all!

But He did it again!

What a heart-break Christ would be today to some well-meaning "promotional committee" or to some "business manager"! It seemed that He always *did* the wrong thing, or *said* the wrong thing, just as He was on the crest of the wave, and at the height of His popularity! He never seemed to understand what was in His own best interests!

Amidst all this popular acclaim, the Lord Jesus Christ went straight to the temple and found ". . . those that sold oxen and sheep and doves, and the changers of money sitting: And when he had made a scourge of small cords, he drove them all out of the temple, and

15

the sheep, and the oxen; and poured out the changers' money, and overthrew the tables; And said unto them that sold doves, Take these things hence; make not my Father's house an house of merchandise" (John 2:14-16).

Had He been prepared to accept "religion" as He found it, and recognize the "status quo," no doubt the Lord Jesus Christ might well have found acceptance, even among the Pharisees; but He was a trouble maker! He dared to cleanse the temple!

Christ did not come to be "accepted," nor was He "looking for a 'job'" in contemporary religion! He came to cleanse the temple—and to do a bigger job than just to cleanse the temple in Jerusalem; He had come to cleanse the temples of men's hearts, that they might be fit again to be "an habitation of God through the Spirit" (Ephesians 2:22).

Challenged to declare by what authority He presumed to disapprove, and by what authority He was prepared to translate His disapproval into action, the Lord Jesus Christ gave this answer: "Destroy this temple, and in three days I will raise it up.—But this spake he of the temple of his body" (John 2:19, 21).

Christ's death and resurrection were to be His mandate, and commitment to Christ for anything less than to be cleansed from sin and inhabited by God, misses the whole point of the cross! He will accept nothing less!

Now when he was in Jerusalem at the passover, in the feast day, many believed in his name, when they saw the miracles which he did. But Jesus did not commit himself unto them, because he knew all men, and needed not that any should testify of man: for he knew what was in man (John 2:23-25).

Although the crowd appeared to have committed themselves to Christ, the quality of their commitment

16

was such that He was not prepared to commit Himself to them!

What is the quality of *your* commitment to Christ?

You may be accepted into membership by the "church," approved by your friends and entrusted with responsible office, but of what possible value can these things be, if your commitment to Christ is such that He is not willing to commit Himself to you? The value of *your* commitment to Christ will only be the measure of *His* commitment to you!

The Lord Jesus Christ is the Truth, and as in all other things "that pertain, unto life and godliness" (II Peter 1:3), He is the Truth about true commitment. He was committed to the Father for all that to which the Father was committed in the Son, and He was supremely confident that the Father who dwelt in Him, was gloriously adequate for all that to which He was committed. We know also that the Saviour's commitment to His Father was such that the Father was completely committed to His Son!

The Lord Jesus Christ refused to be committed to the parochial needs of His own day and generation; He was not committed to the political situation in Palestine, or to the emancipation of the Jewish nation from the Roman yoke! He was not committed to the pressing social problems of His time, nor to one faction as opposed to another, any more than today He is committed to the West against the East, or to the Republicans against the Democrats (as though either were less wicked than the other!). Christ was not even committed to the needs of a perishing world; He was neither unmindful nor unmoved by all these other issues, but as Perfect Man He was committed to His Father, and for that only to which His Father was committed in Him— exclusively!

Then said Jesus unto them. When ye have lifted up the Son of man, then shall ye know that I am he, and that I do

17

nothing of myself; but as my Father hath taught me, I speak these things. And he that sent me is with me: The Father hath not left me alone; for I do always those things that please him (John 8:28, 29).

The Lord Jesus Christ was fully aware from the beginning of that to which the Father was committed in Him, for He was "the Lamb slain from the foundation of the world" (Revelation 13:8). Breaking the bread which pictured His body so soon to be broken, and taking the wine as the symbol of His blood so soon to be shed, He could still look up into His Father's face and say, "Thank You!" He was completely committed, and there were no other issues then for Him to face!

The Lord Jesus Christ knew that before ever men like Wilberforce, Robert Moffat and David Livingstone could be committed to Him for that to which He was to be committed in them—the abolition of slavery and the restoration of human dignity in the equality of all men under God; before ever men like Lord Shaftsbury, Dr. Barnardo and George Mueller could be committed to Him for that for which He was to be committed in them—to gather the ragged, half-starved orphans off the streets of Britain and restore hope to the unwanted; before He could attack the social evils and unschooled ignorance of a wanton nation through the persons of John Wesley and George Whitefield, during the great evangelical awakening of their century, or use Elizabeth Fry to bring about a reformation within an unpitying penal system which left a community of despair to languish, unloved and unmourned, in the vermin-ridden prisons of her land—He the Son of God had first to commit Himself to the Father for that to which the Father was committed in Him!

The basis of His commitment to the Father is the basis upon which the Lord Jesus Christ claims your commitment to Him; you are committed to Him for all that to which He is committed in you—*exclusively*!

18

You are not committed to a church, or to a denomination, or to an organization; as a missionary you are not committed to a Mission Board nor even to a "field," and least of all are you committed to a "need"! You are committed to *Christ,* and for all that to which *Christ is committed in You,* and again I say—*exclusively*!

Thousands of earnest young Christians are challenged with the outworn slogan, "The need is the call!" and are then immediately presented with a dozen different needs, all representing a "call"! When the "invitation" is given, hundreds stand in their confusion, swept to their feet on a wave of sentiment, yet it has been determined on a strictly statistical basis that out of every hundred who stand, not more than three will ever reach the mission field, and of those who do, almost 50 per cent will return home to stay at home by the end of their first term overseas!

Moses mistook the need for the "call," and moved with compassion went out to murder an Egyptian in defence of his brethren, and became useless to God and man for forty years in the backside of the desert, herding a handful of sheep!

Abraham committed himself to the *will* of God, instead of to *God* whose will it was, and in his misguided zeal tried to do God's work man's way! He felt that it was up to him and to Sarai to help God out of His predicament, for Sarai was old and had never borne, for she was barren—so they had a committee meeting! After all, God had said that Abraham was to have a son, and if this was God's will, and he was committed to God's will—a son he must have, at any price!

It was a heavy price that Abraham paid as Hagar, Sarai's maid was summoned, and ill-begotten Ishmael was born to become the father of the Arabs! The Jews in Palestine today, surrounded by hostile Arab nations, reap the bitter harvest still of what was sown in Abraham's self-effort, those many centuries before. Ishmael was the by-product of a false commitment; conceived in sincerity, he was the devil's *reasonable alternative* to *faith!*

When Isaac was born in God's perfect timing, fifteen years later, Ishmael mocked him—and he has been mocking him ever since! ". . . as then he that was born after the flesh persecuted him that was born after the Spirit, even so it is now" (Galatians 4:29); "O that Ishmael might live before thee!" (Genesis 17:18) is still the cry of those who in our own day and generation have yet to learn that ". . . the son of the bondwoman shall not be heir with the son of the freewoman" (Galatians 4:30)—that there is *absolutely no substitute* so far as God is concerned, for God's work done God's way!

When God tested Abraham, and told him to offer up Isaac for a burnt offering, He said, "Take now thy son, thine only son, whom thou lovest, and get thee into the land of Moriah" (Genesis 22:2), and Abraham might have argued with God and said, "But I have *two* sons! What about Ishmael? Isaac is not my *only* son!" Then God would have replied, "So far as I am concerned, only Isaac is your son. I do not recognize Ishmael—he should never have been born!"

The church of Jesus Christ today is plagued with Ishmaels clamoring to be recognized—but God will only honor Isaac, and Isaac's Greater Son! Nothing infuriates the "flesh" more than failure to be recognized—and preaching that exposes it for the wicked counterfeit it is must inevitably be the object of its venom and its wrath! "Too subjective! Unrealistic! Otherworldly! Over-simplified! Mere passivity! Pantheistic mysticism!"—these are some of the epithets with which "Ishmael" still mocks "Isaac"; with which the "flesh" resists the Spirit!

At God's command, Abraham took Isaac, bound him, laid him on the altar he had built, and took his knife to slay him, and with actions far more eloquent

20

than words, said to God by what he did, "You promised me Isaac! I did not see how You could do it, and
in my unbelief and in my folly I produced my Ishmael;
I committed myself to Your *will,* and thought I was
more competent than God. Now You tell me to slay
him, my *only* son Isaac in whom You have promised
that all the families of the earth shall be blessed! O
God, if I slay him, I do not see *how* You can do
it—but now I am committed to *You—exclusively,* and
to all that for which You are committed in me! If slay
him I *must,* then slay him I *will*—even if You have to
raise him from the dead!" (Hebrews 11:17-19), and in
so many words God said to Abraham, "Thank you,
Abraham! That is all I wanted to know—now you can
throw your knife away!"

> Lay not thine hand upon the lad, neither do thou anything
> unto him: for now I know that thou fearest God. By myself
> have I sworn, saith the Lord, for because thou hast done
> this thing, and hast not withheld thy son, thine only son:
> That in blessing I will bless thee, and in multiplying I will
> multiply thy seed as the stars of heaven, and as the sand
> which is upon the sea shore; and thy seed shall possess the
> gate of his enemies; because thou hast obeyed my voice
> (Genesis 22:12, 16-18).

Abraham had learned the secret of true commitment,
and became "the Friend of God" (James 2:23)! This is
reality—and this is discipleship!

It is "godliness in action"! Presenting all that you
are—*nothing,* to all that He is—*everything,* you are
committed to the Lord Jesus Christ *exclusively,* for all
that to which He is committed in you; and you may be
supremely confident that He who dwells in *you* as the
Father dwelt in *Him,* is gloriously adequate for all that
to which He is committed!

Are you prepared for this to be the quality of your
commitment to Christ? If so, then every lesser issue has
been comprehended in the greater. It is now no longer

necessary for me to ask you whether you are prepared to go to the mission field! It is now no longer necessary for me to ask you whether you are prepared to put your bank account at Christ's disposal, or your time, or your home, or face you with any other issue I could think of! You would say to me at once, "These issues now have all been settled—finally, once and for all! If Christ is committed in me to go to the mission field, I am already committed to Him for this! If He is committed in me to use the very last dollar I possess, and every other dollar I shall ever earn, I am already committed to Him for this, and for everything and anything else to which He may be committed in me! There are no more issues for me to face—*only His instructions to obey*! I know too, that *for all His will*, I have *all that He is!* . . . and this is *all* I need to know!"

Indeed it is! . . . for you cannot have *more*!

And you need never have *less*!

2

HOW TO DO THE IMPOSSIBLE

He answered and said unto them, Give ye them to eat (Mark 6:37).

"It is not difficult for man to live the Christian life," somebody once said, "*it is a sheer impossibility!*"

A sheer impossibility, that is, without CHRIST—but for *all that He says,* you have *all that He is,* and that is *all that it takes!*

As we have already seen, this was the lesson that Abraham learned, ". . . being fully persuaded that, what he had promised he was able also to perform" (Romans 4:21), and Mary, too, as we shall see later, "For with God nothing shall be impossible. And Mary said, Behold the handmaid of the Lord; be it unto me according to thy word" (Luke 1:37, 38).

It was this same lesson which the Lord Jesus Christ wished to teach His disciples, but they were very slow to learn—and so are we! "And Jesus, when he came out, saw much people, and was moved with compassion toward them, because they were as sheep not having a shepherd: and he began to teach them many things" (Mark 6:34).

Luther's translation of this last sentence has always been a source of great comfort to me—"He preached a long sermon"!—and it *was* a long sermon! It lasted right on into the evening, and so much so that the disciples began to get quite worried as to what they were going to do with this great crowd of people! "This is a desert place," they said to the Master, "send them away . . . for they have nothing to eat" (Mark 6:35, 36).

To the disciples this seemed to be the only reason-

23

able, sensible thing to do in the face of a situation which threatened to become increasingly embarrassing. There were five thousand men, Matthew records ". . . beside women and children" (Matthew 14:21), and if meetings in those days were anything like meetings in these days, five thousand men *plus* the women and children was a big meeting! The crowd was tired, hot and hungry, and with no prospect of feeding them, there appeared to the disciples to be no alternative but to remind the Lord Jesus Christ of the lateness of the hour, and to say to Him in so many words, "Master, we simply *must* get these people off our hands!"

There is always a *reasonable* alternative to faith!

The Lord Jesus Christ answered them and said, "Give ye them to eat" in other words, "You don't send hungry people away; you feed them!"

"Shall we go and buy two hundred pennyworth of bread, and give them to eat?" (Mark 6:37), asked the bewildered disciples, "Master, that's a sheer impossibility!"

"Exactly! To you it is a sheer impossibility," the Lord Jesus Christ might well have replied, "and that is why we are going to do it; I am going to show you how to do the impossible!"

The Christian life can only be explained in terms of Jesus Christ, and if your life as a Christian can still be explained in terms of *you—your* personality, *your* willpower, *your* gift, *your* talent, *your* money, *your* courage, *your* scholarship, *your* dedication, *your* sacrifice, or *your* anything—then although you may *have* the Christian life, you are not yet living it!

If the way you live your life as a Christian can be explained in terms of *you*, what have you to offer to the man who lives next door? The way he lives his life can be explained in terms of *him*, and so far as he is concerned, you happen to be "religious"—but he is not! "Christianity" may be *your* hobby, but it is not his, and there is nothing about the way you practice it

24

which strikes him as at all remarkable! There is nothing about you which leaves him guessing, and nothing commendable of which he does not feel himself equally capable without the inconvenience of becoming a Christian!

It is only when your quality of life *baffles* the neighbors that you are likely to *impress* them! It has got to become patently obvious to others that the kind of life you are living is not only *highly commendable,* but that it is beyond all *human explanation!* That it is beyond the consequences of man's capacity to *imitate,* and however little they may understand this, clearly the consequence only of God's capacity to *reproduce Himself* in you!

In a nutshell, this means that your fellow-men must become convinced that the Lord Jesus Christ of whom you speak, is essentially Himself the ingredient of the Life you live!

How did Christ feed the five thousand? To discover this, we need to turn to the record found in the sixth chapter of John's Gospel, for here it is as though the Apostle takes a magnifying glass and allows us to examine the story in greater detail. "When Jesus then lifted up his eyes, and saw a great company come unto him, he saith unto Philip, Whence shall we buy bread, that these may eat? And this he said to prove him: for he himself knew what he would do" (John 6:5, 6).

Was Christ seeking advice when He asked Philip this question? Was He at a loss to know what to do? Most certainly not, for "He Himself knew what He would do." He knew *exactly* what He would do! He always does, no matter with what situation He may be confronted, at any time, and anywhere! Nothing ever takes Him by surprise, and nothing shocks Him; He is *never* baffled—*never* bewildered! He is the God who declares "the end from the beginning," and upon whose Head no emergency can ever break! As I once heard a noted Christian psychologist, Dr. Cramer, remark, "The Lord

Jesus Christ was completely 'panic-proof' "—and He still is!

Are you?

This will be singularly characteristic of you, if you are really enjoying the Life of the Lord Jesus Christ; you, too, will be "panic-proof"! Yours will be the "peace of God, which passeth all understanding" (Philippians 4:7)—that is to say, peace which in the light of all the circumstances, is beyond all human explanation!

Christ was not seeking advice when He asked Philip this question, nor was He trying to discover anything *about* Philip, for again and again occasions are recorded in the Gospels, where the Lord Jesus Christ replied to a person's *thoughts*. He knew everything there was to know about Philip's heart, and a whole lot more than Philip knew himself, as He knows everything there is to know about your heart and mine! "And not a creature exists that is concealed from His sight, but all things are open *and* exposed, naked *and* defenseless to the eyes of Him with Whom we have to do" (Hebrews 4:13, *Amplified New Testament*).

Then why did Christ ask this question?

He asked this question because He wanted Philip to discover something about himself! He wanted him to discover the utter poverty of his experience of Christ— how very far short he fell of living miraculously! Nor was it for Philip alone to make this discovery, but for all of His disciples. "Philip answered him, Two hundred pennyworth of bread is not sufficient for them, that everyone of them may take a little (John 6:7).

With what then was Philip reckoning? Was it with the presence and power of the Lord Jesus Christ? No! Just with the money in the bag! Beyond that for him, in this situation, there was no further horizon; so far as Philip was concerned, for all the difference that the presence of Christ made to the problem, He might just as well have been dead!

Had a materialistically minded atheist been consulted

in the face of this dilemma, the first question he would have asked would have been, "How much money do you have?" What then would have been the difference between Philip's out-look and that of an unbelieving atheist? There would have been *no* difference!

Philip had not learned to *reckon* with Christ! Because to him their financial resources were all-important, Jesus Christ was unimportant! There was nothing about the kind of life he was living as an apostle which could not have been given its "dollar-equivalent"!

What are *you* reckoning with? Are you *really* reckoning with Christ? Upon what basis have you evaluated the many different situations which have arisen within the last twenty-four hours, before taking this book in your hand and reading these pages? Did you take the Lord Jesus Christ into account—or did you consider Him to be irrelevant?

Remember that it is precisely in those areas of your life in which you have not considered Christ to be relevant, in which as yet you have not repented. In these areas you are still trying to be adequate without Him—trying to be the "cause" of your own "effect"; and if *you* are the cause, there will certainly be nothing miraculous about the effect!

In your disillusionment, you may well try, as the disciples did, to get the situation "off your hands," convinced that you are as inadequate with Christ as without Him! Then you *will* be miserable! Better not visit the neighbors *that* day!

The Lord Jesus Christ said, "How many loaves have ye? go and see" (Mark 6:38), and when they went, they found Andrew arguing with a small boy! I can imagine that the conversation ran something like this:

"It's kind of you, laddie, and I will tell the Master that you offered, but I don't think we should disturb Him now; you see, He's busy—and in any case, five loaves and two fishes just aren't enough to go around!

27

That's just about your size—*you* could wrap yourself round that! But thanks again, lad—thanks a lot! I'll tell the Master, I promise!"

Indignantly the boy replied, "I don't care whether I've got *five* loaves, or *fifty* loaves, or *five hundred* loaves, or *five thousand* loaves— *that* does not matter! *Please take me to that man*! That is *all* that matters!"

At that moment the others arrived on the scene, and maybe if the Master had not sent them, Andrew never would have brought that boy to the Lord Jesus; even when he did, it was only to apologize! "One of his disciples, Andrew, Simon Peter's brother, saith unto him, There is a lad here, which hath five barley loaves, and two small fishes: but what are they among so many?" (John 6: 8, 9).

Andrew, I am sure, was not unkind to the boy! I believe from the record that we have of him in the Gospels, that Andrew was of a particularly kindly disposition, and maybe that was why the lad felt at liberty to speak to him; perhaps a friendly smile had given him the invitation! Andrew, I believe, had a face like a door-mat—one that has "Welcome" woven into it! Some folk wonder why it is that no one ever comes to them for counsel—they have faces like a notice on the gate, "Beware of the Dog"!

Be that as it may, and kind as he may have been, what was Andrew reckoning with? Was he reckoning with the presence and the power of Christ? No! Just with five barley loaves and two small fishes, and because these to him were all-important, Jesus Christ was unimportant!

On the other hand, because to this small boy the Lord Jesus Christ was *all-important*, the vastness of the need and the poverty of supply were totally *unimportant*! He had already learned the secret of living miraculously, for the lad had learned in his own way to *reckon with Christ*!

This is always a precious story to me, for the Lord

28

Jesus Himself "knew what He would do" long before Andrew spoke to that small boy, or ever anyone else had recognized the potential in him. Christ knew his heart and had already chosen him!

In *every* crowd there is always *one* at least whose heart He knows, and whom He has already chosen! To *discern* that one, and to bring that one—without apology—is the holy art of soul-winning; ". . . and he that winneth souls is wise" (Proverbs 11:30)!

It will not always be the most prominent, nor even the most promising—maybe just a lad with a lunch-bag, and a twinkle in his eye! "And Jesus took the loaves; and when he had given thanks, he distributed to the disciples, and the disciples to them that were set down; and likewise of the fishes as much as they would" (John 6:11).

Whatever second thoughts some "learned theologians" may have had about the memorable events which took place on that exciting day, those who were present and were witnesses were obviously in no doubt at all, as to what had really happened, for " . . . those men, when they had seen the miracle which Jesus did, said, This is of a truth that prophet that should come into the world" (John 6:14). They recognized the fact at once, as they watched the Lord Jesus Christ at work, that here was a Man for whose activities there could be absolutely no explanation at all, apart from God!

There are those of course, who would have you accept "the little paper-bag" theory! They would seek to persuade you that when the crowd saw the unselfishness of the little boy, taking out his lunch-pack and being willing to share his five loaves and two small fishes with the multitude, they were so touched and ashamed that suddenly about five-thousand "little paper-bags" appeared—and everyone began to share with everyone else what till then they had been hiding underneath their shirts!

Isn't that sweet?

Some folks call this "scholarship," and grant "doctorates" on the strength of it! The twelve baskets might have been better used to gather up the litter, than to gather up the fragments that remained!

If you only have a "little paper-bag god," then you must content yourself with "little paper-bag miracles"—but with *our God* "... nothing shall be impossible" (Luke 1:37)!

> When they were filled, he said unto his disciples, Gather up the fragments that remain, that nothing be lost. Therefore they gathered them together, and filled twelve baskets *with the fragments of the five barley loaves*, which remained over and above unto them that had eaten (John 6:12, 13, *italics used for emphasis only*).

There was a secret to the miracle which the Lord Jesus Christ performed; a secret which He wanted to share with His disciples, and which He wants to share with you, too! To miss this, is to miss the object of the exercise, the lesson to be learned! It is at the very heart of the mystery of Godliness! It is written that "Jesus took the loaves; and *when he had given thanks,* he distributed to the disciples, (*italics for emphasis only*). Whom did Christ thank? Did He thank Himself? God as God certainly has no one to thank but Himself, and Jesus Christ was God! It is quite obvious that the Lord Jesus Christ as the Son, gave thanks to His Father as God, and in His perfect role as Perfect Man, relentlessly refused to be the "cause of His own effect"!

As the Creator God, there is absolutely no doubt but that Christ could Himself have fed the five thousand, or for that matter, five hundred times five thousand—but then He would not have been behaving as Man, He would have been behaving as God; and as we shall discover later, had He both *been* and *behaved* as God, no one would have seen Him! No one has seen God at any time!

As the "only begotten Son" Christ "declared" the

Father (John 1:18) in all that He said, in all that He did, and in all that He was; and as I shall remind you yet again, the Lord Jesus said, ". . . the Father that dwelleth in me, He doeth the works" (John 14:10).

So who fed the five thousand? The Father through the Son!

In spite of His eternal equality with the Father and with the Holy Spirit in the Trinity of the Deity, the Lord Jesus Christ for our sakes made Himself *nothing,* (Philippians 2:7, *New English Bible*), that the Father might be *everything,* and be glorified in Him! In an attitude of total dependence, He exercised toward the Father as God that perfect "faith-love" relationship for which man by Christ Himself had been created!

Confronted by this hungry multitude of people, Christ deliberately subjected Himself to the limitations which He as the creative Word, had imposed upon man as His own creation—He exposed the situation to His Father, and in humble dependence upon His adequacy said quite simply, "Thank You"—and then He reckoned with the Father as He divided the loaves and the fishes!

That is how to do the impossible!

When the Lord Jesus Christ raised Lazarus from the dead, how did He do it?

"Take ye away the stone," He said to Martha, the sister of him that was dead, but she said to Him, "Lord, by this time he stinketh: for he hath been dead four days" (John 11:39). Clearly, by any natural standards, the situation was impossible; yet Christ said to Martha, "Said I not unto thee, that, if thou wouldest believe, thou shouldest see the glory of God?" (John 11:40). Once more the Father was to be glorified in and through the Son! "Then they took away the stone from the place where the dead was laid" (John 11:41).

Christ on this occasion was confronted by a man four days dead, and with all the indisputable evidences of decay, as He stood before the open cave; was this to

31

be His problem? Was His the right to challenge the awful finality of death? The *power* indeed He had, for He was God, but not the *right,* for He was Man! "For even Christ pleased not himself" (Romans 15:3).

How then did Christ do the impossible and raise this man from the dead?

Christ raised Lazarus from the dead just as He had fed the five thousand! He exposed the situation to His Father, and in humble dependence upon His adequacy He said quite simply, "Thank You"—and then reckoned with the Father as He cried with a loud voice, "Lazarus, come forth. And he that was dead came forth, . . ." (John 11:43, 44).

It was just as simple as that! "And Jesus lifted up his eyes, and said, Father, I thank thee that thou hast heard me. And I knew that thou hearest me always: but because of the people which stand by I said it, that they may believe that thou hast sent me" (John 11:41, 42).

Christ sought then, as He had sought by the feeding of the five thousand, to demonstrate the principle by which He lived His supernatural life as Man on earth; that you with all men might believe that He was the "Sent One," and His Father the "Sender," and that you might know and believe that as the *Father* sent *Him,* so *He* sends *you*—to live miraculously!

"Verily, verily, I say unto you, He that believeth on me, the works that I do shall he do also; and greater works than these shall he do; because I go unto my Father" (John 14:12).

The Lord Jesus Christ wants to be to you now, all that the Father was to Him then—GOD; if only you will be to Him now, all that He was to the Father then—MAN!

Have you learned to expose *every* situation to the Lord Jesus Christ in humble dependence upon His adequacy, and simply to say, "Thank You," and then to reckon with Him as you act to meet that situation?

By the feeding of the five thousand in humble dependence on the Father, the Lord Jesus Christ showed His disciples how to do the impossible, and to live miraculously!

How much did His disciples learn?

Nothing!

3

I AM—THOU ART!

For they considered not the miracle of the loaves: for their heart was hardened (Mark 6:52).

"*Get them off our hands!* Send them away, for they have nothing to eat!" That was the pitiful cry of the disciples as they came in panic to the Lord Jesus Christ; but instead, He *fed* the hungry multitude, *and got His disciples off His hands*!

It is one of the hardest lessons for us to learn, that none of us are ever indispensable to God, but God is *always* indispensable to us! "And those that did eat of the loaves were about five thousand men. And straightway he constrained his disciples to get into the ship, and to go to the other side before Bethsaida, while he sent away the people" (Mark 6:44, 45).

Why did He send His disciples away? He sent them away because they had learned *nothing*—absolutely *nothing*! "For they failed to consider *or* understand [the teaching and meaning of the miracle of] the loaves; [in fact] their hearts had grown callous—had become dull and had lost the power of understanding" (Mark 6:52, *Amplified New Testament*)—"... their heart was hardened"!

Called to be apostles, and the closest companions of the Saviour during His earthly ministry, they lived and worked and walked and talked with Him; they shared His platform, basked in His lime-light, and had a name to be His most devoted followers! Yes, they were *big names*—but they were *big names* with *hard hearts*!

To hold office does not in itself make a man spiritual! Unfortunately, all too often it is the *unspiritual* who

34

fight and edge their way into office, where the "flesh" can indulge its insatiable appetite for position and power; for the "flesh" loves to be recognized, consulted, honored, admired and obeyed!

You may be a bishop, a pastor, the church secretary, an elder or deacon; you may be the president, principal or dean of a college; you may be chairman of some mission board or the field director as the senior missionary on the field; you may hold any office of any kind, however distinguished it may be—*and still have a hard heart*! Where this is the case, and where there is *real* business to be done, you must not be surprised if Christ gets *you* off His hands too,—unless and until you repent!

> God is not impressed with the positions that men hold *and* He is not partial *and* recognizes no external distinctions (Galatians 2:6, *Amplified New Testament*).
> Because thou sayest, I am rich, and increased with goods, and have need of nothing; and knowest not that thou art wretched, and miserable, and poor, and blind, and naked: . . . As many as I love, I rebuke and chasten: be zealous therefore, and repent (Revelation 3:17, 19).

Do not allow the poverty of self-sufficiency to rob you of the miraculous! It is a particularly subtle form of conceit which denies to God the possibility of doing what you consider to be beyond the bounds of your own carnal self-esteem!

How patient Christ was with His disciples! Having learned nothing, they were given the same lesson all over again, but in another setting. A setting, indeed, which was little to the liking of the disciples themselves, for having been sent away, they found themselves ". . . in the midst of the sea, tossed with waves: for the wind was contrary" (Matthew 14:24)!

With their backs bent to the oars, perspiration pouring down their faces, and every muscle aching, they battled against the storm! Darkness had already fallen,

35

and the shore-line had long been lost to sight, and as the mountainous waves beat into the little boat, threat-ening to swamp it and send it to the bottom, the disciples began to wonder whether they would ever reach their destination! "And in the fourth watch of the night Jesus went unto them, . . ."—doing what?

Doing the impossible! ". . . walking on the sea" (Matthew 14:25)!

How did the Lord Jesus Christ do the impossible? How did He walk on the water? He did this as He had fed the five thousand, and as He had raised Lazarus from the dead! He *reckoned* with His Father—just one step at a time—and for every step He took He said, "Thank You, Father!"

Christ demonstrated to His disciples that everything that threatened to be *over their heads,* His Father had already put *under His feet!*

What is it that is threatening *you*? What makes you afraid? What is it from which you are running away? Is there something that seems about to swamp *your* little boat—that baffles, beats and bewilders you? Here is *good news* for you! There is nothing which could ever threaten to be over your head, which He does not already have under His feet—and He is waiting for you to share His victory! "And when the disciples saw Him walking on the sea, they were terrified, and said, It is a ghost! And they screamed out with fright. But instantly He spoke to them, saying, Take courage! I AM; stop being afraid!" (Matthew 14:26, 27, *Amplified New Testament*).

They thought they had seen a ghost! A Man walking on the water—that is impossible! But the Lord Jesus said, "I AM: stop being afraid!" In so many words, Christ said to His disciples. "I AM;—all that you could *ever* need, at *any* time, in *any* storm and all that I AM, you HAVE! Stop being frightened!" "And Peter answered him and said, Lord, if it be thou, bid me come unto thee on the water" (Matthew 14:28).

"Master," Peter might have said, ". . . if it be *Thou,* then please put under *my* feet what is already under *Thy* feet!" You can almost imagine the smile there must have been on the face of the Master! "Why, Peter! That is all I have been waiting for! I have simply been waiting for *you* to reckon with Me, as *I* reckon with My Father! Come on!—Come!"

At the command of the Lord Jesus Christ, Peter stepped over the side, "And when Peter was come down out of the ship," what do you think he did? He did the *impossible!*—". . . he walked on the water, to go to Jesus" (Matthew 14:29)!

One step at a time, and for every step he took, you could almost have heard Peter crying in his excitement, "This is wonderful, Lord! Thank You! Thank You, Lord!—This is tremendous; this is an entirely new experience for me, I have never walked on water before! Thank You, Lord! Thank You!"

As Peter kept his eyes upon the Saviour, and related his situation to Christ for every step he took, he shared the victory of his Lord! The impossible became possible!

Suddenly an unkind wave slapped Peter on the face from one side, and yet another hit him from the other side, and he almost lost his balance! His attention was distracted from Christ, and once more he became aware of the howling of the wind and the swelling of the waters; he stopped relating the situation *to the Lord* and began again to relate the situation to *himself,* and began immediately to think, *I can't do this*! *A man can't walk on water—that's impossible*! . . . and he was quite right! Peter began to go down for a ducking, and ". . . cried, saying, Lord, save me" (Matthew 14:30)!

The Lord Jesus Christ immediately stretched forth His hand and caught him; He recaptured Peter's attention and once more He put the threatening waters beneath his feet, and they walked *together* until they

37

were come into the ship, and ". . . the wind ceased" (Matthew 14:32). The exercise was over!

What do you think Christ said to Peter? Perhaps you think He should have congratulated him! "Peter, I just want you to know how immensely I appreciated your *tremendous* faith! The way you got out of that boat and walked toward Me was a masterpiece! I *must* congratulate you; I haven't seen such a great faith in a long time!" Is that what Christ said? Oh no! Far from it! Instead He said to him, "O thou of little faith, wherefore didst thou doubt?" (Matthew 14:31). In so many words He said, "It is not *difficult,* Peter, to do the impossible! It is *inevitable* so long as you reckon with *Me*! Why did you stop reckoning? I can't *congratulate* you, Peter. I'm just sorry that your faith was so small!"

The lesson, however, was not in vain! "Then they that were in the ship came and worshipped him, saying, Of a truth thou art the Son of God" (Matthew 14:33).

In the midst of the storm, when everything was against them, the Lord Jesus Christ appeared and said, "I AM; stop being afraid," and now at last they had learned to say, "Of a truth *thou art* the Son of God!" If there is nothing else that you remember of all that has been written in this book, this in itself would comprehend the whole relationship of God to man, and man to God: ". . . for he that cometh to God must believe that he is"—"Thou art"—". . . and that he is a rewarder of them that diligently seek him"—"I AM"! (Hebrews 11:6). All that you could ever need at any time, in *any* storm; "and all that I AM," He says, "you *have*!"

It may be that your need is still that of a sinner seeking forgiveness; you need to be redeemed, and you are still trying to find your way back to God and godliness. Christ is saying to you now, as He said to His disciples of old in the Upper Room, after He was risen from the dead, "Behold my hands and my feet, that it is I myself" (Luke 24:39); in other words, "I AM—all that a guilty sinner needs! The wounds in My hands and My feet are the hall-marks of My Saviourhood; put your trust in Me, and I will save you!"

All you need to say to Him is this, "Lord Jesus—*Thou art*! For *me*—just what I need! *My* Saviour and *my* Redeemer—for ever!"

> Behold Him there, the risen Lamb!
> My perfect, spotless righteousness,
> The great unchangeable I AM,
> The King of glory and of grace.

You will be redeemed, and He will give you *life*; by the gift of His indwelling Holy Spirit, Jesus Christ will give you *His* Life, and this is what it means to "*live* in the Spirit"; but "If we live in the Spirit, let us also walk in the Spirit" (Galatians 5:25), and *this* is what it means to "*walk* in the Spirit"—to take *one* step at a time, and for every new situation into which every new step takes you, no matter what it may be, to hear Christ saying to your heart, "I AM!"—and then to look up into His face by faith and say, "*Thou art*! That is all I need to know Lord, and I thank Thee; for Thou art never *less* than adequate!"

Thus to walk is to experience with Paul the Apostle:

I know how to be abased *and* live humbly in straightened circumstances, and I know also how to enjoy plenty *and* live in abundance. I have learned in any and all circumstances, the secret of facing every situation, whether well-fed or going hungry, having a sufficiency *and* to spare or going without *and* being in want. I have strength for all things in Christ who empowers me—I am ready for anything and equal to anything through Him Who infuses inner strength into me, [that is, I am self-sufficient in Christ's sufficiency] (Philippians 4:12, 13, *Amplified New Testament*).

Without this kind of faith it is impossible to please God, for without this kind of faith, it is impossible for God to reproduce His character in you—and that is godliness!

39

True godliness leaves the world convinced beyond a shadow of a doubt, that the only explanation for *you,* is *Jesus Christ*—to whose eternally unchanging and altogether adequate "I Aм!" your heart has learned to say with unshatterable faith, "*Thou art!*"

That is really all you need to know!

"And all of us, as with unveiled face, [because we] continue to behold *and* to reflect like mirrors the glory of the Lord, are constantly being transformed into [His very own] image in ever increasing splendor *and* from one degree of glory to another; [for this comes] from the Lord [Who is the] Spirit" (II Corinthians 3:18, *Amplified New Testament*).

4

THE NATURE OF THE MYSTERY

*Without controversy great is the mystery of godliness:
God was manifest in the flesh . . . (I Timothy 3:16).*

Godliness is a mystery! Fail to grasp this fact and
you will never understand the nature of godliness.

God did not create you to have just an ape-like
capacity to imitate God. There would be no mystery in
that, nor would this lift you morally much above the
status of a monkey or a parrot! The capacity to imitate
is vested in the one who imitates, and does not derive
from, nor necessarily share the motives of the person
being imitated, who remains passive and impersonal to
the act of imitation.

The kindness and sheer generosity of a certain individual may be an act of pure benevolence, a genuine,
selfless expression of the love of God. You may be
tempted to imitate this person's act, to reproduce it in
kind, or even to out-match it, but *your motives may be
entirely evil,* though the act identical!

Pride may persuade you "not to be out-done!" Jeal-
ousy may compel you to prove that the other party "is
not the only pebble on the beach!" You may resent the
gratitude or affection or respect that the other person,
however unintentionally, has justly earned and
deserved, or you may feel that the regard in which the
other is now held may lessen your own influence over
the future course of events!

In this case, you may deceive the undiscerning with
your generosity, and achieve your ends, but your "generosity" will not be godliness—your "generosity" will
be *sin!*

In direct contrast to this, godliness—or God-likeness—is the direct and exclusive consequence of *God's* activity in man. Not the consequence of your capacity to imitate God, but the consequence of God's capacity to *reproduce Himself* in you! This is the nature of the mystery!

Remove the mystery or try to explain it away, and the result must inevitably be disastrous, for you will no longer be anchored to anything absolute; you will be at liberty to choose your own God—the object of your own imitation; and your "godliness" will be the measure of your conformity to the object of your choice.

This, in point of fact, is what has been happening all through human history since Adam repudiated the basic principles of his own humanity, and decided to go it alone—without God! Man may hide from God—as Adam did—but still the voice of God pursues him, echoing within the spiritual vacuum of his home-sick, godless soul with all the relentless persistency of a love that never fails, crying, "Son of Adam, where *art* thou?—Where *art* thou?—Where *art* thou?"

This is what makes even the most degenerate individual incurably religious, even though his "religion" may be most horrible in character and assume the most hideous of forms—sometimes even disguising itself as a political creed as in the national socialism of Adolf Hitler, or as in the atheistic communism of Karl Marx, which for all their political flavor and advertised contempt for religion, *are none the less religions in themselves*.

It is one of the subtleties of Satan which causes men to flee from God and seek to silence His voice *in the very practice of religion*.

So it is that man, to suit his own convenience, has reduced God to a theological formula, an ethical code, or political program, a theatrical performance in a religious setting, the hero worship of some vivid personality of noble—or doubtful—reputation, or some dreamed-

up image of his own better self; everything from a
white cow to the wind in the trees, or a "Christless
Christianity" has been and still remains the object of
man's idolatry!

The moment you come to realize that only *God* can
make a man godly, you are left with no option but to
find God, and to *know* God, and to let God *be* God in
you and through you, whoever He may be—and this
will leave you with no margin for picking and choos-
ing—for there is only *one* God, and He is absolute, and
He made you expressly for *Himself*!

Beware lest even as a Christian, you fall into Satan's
trap! You may have *found* and come to *know* God in
the Lord Jesus Christ, receiving Him sincerely as your
Redeemer, yet if you do not enter in the mystery of
godliness and allow God to *be* in you the origin of His
own image, you will seek to be godly by submitting
yourself to external rules and regulations, and by conformity to behavior patterns imposed upon you by the
particular Christian society which you have chosen, and
in which you hope to be found "acceptable." You will
in this way perpetuate the pagan habit of practicing
religion in the energy of the "flesh," and in the very
pursuit of righteousness commit idolatry in honoring
"Christianity" more than Christ!

If then you have died with Christ to material ways of looking at things and have escaped from the world's crude and
elemental notions and teachings of externalism, why do you
live as if you still belong to the world?—Why do you submit to rules and regulations? [Such as], Do not handle
[this], Do not taste [that], Do not even touch [them],

Referring to things all of which perish with being used. To
do this is to follow human precepts and doctrines. Such
[practices] have indeed the outward appearance [that popu-
larly passes] for wisdom, in promoting self-imposed rigor
of devotion and delight in self-humiliation and severity of
discipline of the body, but they are of no value in checking

43

the indulgence of the flesh—the lower nature. [Instead, they do not honor God] but serve only to indulge the flesh (Colossians 2:20-23, *Amplified New Testament*).

GOD CANNOT BE SEEN

"And God said, let us make man in our image, after our likeness: . . . so God created man in his own image, in the image of God created he him . . ." (Genesis 1:26 and 27). This does not mean that man was created physically in the shape of God, nor that God looks like a man. We do not know what God looks like, for "No man hath seen God at any time . . ." (John 1:18). The Bible declares expressly that God is *invisible,* "Now unto the king eternal, immortal, invisible, the only wise God, be honour and glory for ever and ever. Amen . . . Who only hath immortality, dwelling in the light which no man can approach unto; whom no man hath seen, nor can see: to whom be honour and power everlasting. Amen" (I Timothy 1:17 and 6:16).

The Bible is equally emphatic concerning the absolute deity of the Son, and His equality with the Father which the Lord Jesus Christ never once repudiated; yet no man has seen God at any time—did no one ever see Jesus Christ? This is part of the mystery! "God was manifest in the flesh . . ." (I Timothy 3:16), and further, ". . . the only begotten Son, which is in the bosom of the Father, he hath declared him" (John 1:18).

Philip said: "Lord, show us the Father, and it sufficeth us." And the Lord Jesus replied, "Have I been so long time with you and yet hast thou not known me, Philip? He that hath seen me hath seen the Father; and how sayest thou then, show us the Father?" (John 14:8 and 9). To reconcile this statement of the Lord Jesus, and the fact of His own deity, with the fact that no man has seen God at any time, would seem at first to present an insuperable problem, for we are presented with the baffling conclusion that in spite of His total

44

equality within the Trinity of Deity, it was possible, nineteen hundred years ago, for men on earth to look into the face of the Son, see the Father, and yet not see God!

The solution to this mystery, as I trust you will discover, is really remarkably simple—for in Jesus Christ Himself it has become an open secret, and one which He invites *you* to share with Him!

It is of paramount importance, from the very outset, that we recognize the fact that when the Lord Jesus Christ was here on earth, He could *be* God and *be* man at one and the same time, but He could not *behave* as God and *behave* as man at one and the same time.

Allow me to explain a little, for to understand this is calculated to bring you untold comfort and encouragement, and to give you an entirely new concept of the Christian life, and a richer, fuller experience of Christ Himself.

Man was created in such a way that he could bear the *image* of God without God Himself becoming *visible,* so that not his *physical form,* but his *capacity to behave* was designed to be the means through which God intended to express His nature and His character. As we have already seen, however, this godliness or God-likeness was not to have been an imitation of God *by* man, but the direct result of the activity of God *in* man. In other words—God Himself behaving in and through *you!*

Man's behavior as the *effect,* was to have been the result of God's behavior as the *cause.* The former was to have been the "brightness" or the "out-shining" of the latter's glory, the "express *image*" of His Person! (Hebrews 1:3) The image was to have been *visible,* while the Person still remained *invisible!*

Had the Lord Jesus Christ been the source of His own godliness, as He could have been, He would have been *behaving* as God only—both *cause* and *effect*—but the result would not have been visible! He had the

45

right to behave as God only—for He *was* and *is* God but He could not then have behaved as man: He would not in point of fact have been godly, or "Godlike," He would just simply have been God; but "no man hath seen God at any time," so that had He in this world both *been* and *behaved* as God, no one would have seen Him! In order to be seen, He had to be made "in the likeness of men" and be found "in fashion as a man" (Philippians 2:7 and 8), and *behave* as man.

To perform in perfection on earth the role for which Christ as God had created man, He had of His own free volition to accept the limitations imposed upon His own creature, and to allow the Father, *as God,* to be the origin of all His own behavior *as Man,* so that His godliness as Man was derived directly and exclusively from the activity of the Father in and through the Son.

In His sinless and perfect humanity Christ became "the sole expression of the glory of God—the light-being, the outraying of the divine—and He is the perfect imprint and very image of God's nature . . ." (Hebrews 1:3, *Amplified New Testament*). Or as Paul declares: "He is the exact likeness of the unseen God—the visible representation of the invisible . . ." (Colossians 1:15, *Amplified New Testament*).

This will help us to understand more fully what the Bible means when it says, "He humbled Himself, and became obedient . . ." (Philippians 2:8). Not simply that He accepted the physical limitations of the human body, but that He adopted an attitude of total dependence upon the Father, and denied Himself the right to exercise all those prerogatives of deity which were undoubtedly His by virtue of the fact that He *was* both God and man, at one and the same time. He deliberately made Himself of "no reputation," and consistently refused to be the "cause" of His own "effect," declaring emphatically: "I can of mine own self do nothing" (John 5:30).

To use a simple illustration, no man has seen electricity at any time, yet an electric light bulb is so designed that whenever it receives the invisible electric current, *expression* is given to the *invisible* in terms of *light*.

It would not be true to say that the *bulb* is giving light, for it has no power to do so apart from the current which it receives: its behavior as a "light-giver" is the direct and exclusive consequence of the activity of the electricity in it and through it. The current is the *cause*, light is the *effect*, and though you can see the effect, you still cannot see the cause, though both represent the same source of energy!

You can enjoy the light, but you still cannot say that you have seen electricty! You can only say that you have seen a pure expression of it. In the same way, your behavior was intended by God to be a pure expression of His divine nature, though He remains unseen, and you can no more produce this effect *of yourself*, than a bulb can produce light of *itself*! Try, and you will soon be exhausted, and at best you will only produce a shabby imitation of the real thing. It may impress *you*, but it certainly will not impress anyone else!

It is only the Spirit of God acting within you, who can ever enable you to behave as God intended you to behave! "According as His divine power hath given unto us all things that pertain unto life and godliness through the knowledge of Him that hath called us to glory and virtue" (II Peter 1:3). His divine power is all that it takes to be godly—*but it takes nothing less*!

In other words, it takes *God* to be a *man*! Man, that is, as God intended man to be! God created man to be inhabited *by* God *for* God! "In Him was life, and the life was the light of men" (John 1:4). The Light depended on the Life! Once the Life was removed, the Light went out, for the one was the consequence of the other, and man was plunged into the abysmal darkness of his own spiritual bankruptcy!

What of the "image"? Without a *cause* there was no

effect, and the attributes of godliness gave way to the anarchy of godlessness! "God looked down from heaven upon the children of men, to see if there were any that did understand, that did seek God. Every one of them is gone back: they are altogether become filthy; there is none that doeth good, no, not one" (Psalm 53:2 and 3).

That is why a spiritual regeneration, or New Birth— "renewing of the Holy Spirit" (Titus 3:5)—is absolutely imperative if man is to "put on the new nature (the regenerate self) created in God's image, (God-like) in true righteousness and holiness" (Ephesians 4:24, *Amplified New Testament*).

GOD CANNOT BE TEMPTED

"Let no man say when he is tempted, I am tempted of God: for God cannot be tempted with evil, neither tempteth he any man:" (James 1:13). If God cannot be tempted with evil, and Jesus Christ was God, how could He be tempted? "For we have not an high Priest which cannot be touched with the feeling of our infirmities; but was in all points tempted like as we are, yet without sin" (Hebrews 4:15).

It is no explanation to suggest that though *tempted* the Lord Jesus Christ was not tempted with *evil,* but only in the sense that He was tested—for the statement, "yet without sin," clearly indicates that the nature of the temptation was such that it would have led to sin had it not been resisted. Indeed, we may safely assume that the temptations were as sinister and wicked and painful as anything that the devil could devise, and for this very reason "in that He himself hath suffered being tempted, He is able to succour those that are tempted" (Hebrews 2:18).

This then is also part of the mystery, that inherent in His willingness to be made Man, was the willingness of the Lord Jesus Christ to be made subject to temptation,

48

for strange as it may seem, inherent in man's capacity to be godly is man's very capacity to sin! This may not at first be obvious, but we shall return to it at the appropriate time.

In the meantime, we are left with no alternative but to recognize the fact that it was not as *God* that Christ was tempted, but as *Man*; that the limitations inherent in His ability to be tempted, were the same limitations which He had so willingly accepted as being inherent in His ability, though Creator, to play the role of man as His creature and thereby to become the Visible Representation of the Invisible.

It has been shown that the primary limitation imposed upon you as man, in order that you may be in the likeness of your Maker and bear the image of the Invisible, is that of total dependence upon God—in that your behavior, to be godly, must derive directly and exclusively from God's activity in you and through you. Any activity, therefore, in which you may engage, no matter how nobly conceived, which does not stem from this humble attitude of dependence upon God, violates the basic principles of your true humanity and the role for which you were created. By independence (or the absence of faith), you eliminate *God,* and substitute *yourself*, to become both cause and effect—the source of your own "godliness," but only God has the right to be the source of His own godliness, so that however unwittingly, you are acting as your own God!

You will still believe or pretend that you are worshiping God; but as the object of your imitation, even Christ Himself may only be an excuse for worshiping your own ability to imitate—an ability vested in yourself, and this is the basis of all self-righteousness!

It is startling to discover that even God may be used as an excuse for worshipping yourself, and demonstrates again the satanic genius for distorting truth, and deceiving man—for it was to this temptation that Adam and Eve fell in the garden!

Satan said, "For God doth know that in the day that you eat thereof, then your eyes shall be opened, and ye shall be as gods, knowing good and evil" (Genesis 3:5). Satan succeeded in introducing into human experience an attitude toward God which he himself had already adopted, one of arrogant self-sufficiency, at once hostile to God, repudiating both the indispensability of the Creator to the creature, and the moral responsibility of the creature to the Creator.

In so many words, Satan persuaded man that he could be God-like without being God-conscious; that he had an adequate capacity in himself for being *good,* without the necessity of having *God*; that he could be righteous in his own right, *morally adult* without the need of being *spiritually alive*! In short, that man could be independent—both cause and effect!

Revelation 4:11 declares, "Thou art worthy, O Lord, to receive glory and honour and power: for thou hast created all things, and for thy pleasure they are and were created." If, then, man is to be true to the purpose of his creation, his primary responsibility will be to please God; but the Bible declares emphatically that "without faith it is impossible to please Him" (Hebrews 11:6). So that the first requirement in man, if he is to please God, is *faith.*

Faith involves something more than an academic nod! It involves that total dependence upon God which produces divine action in man.

Perhaps you may say, "Very well, I understand that faith is essential for those preoccupied with pleasing God, but I am *not* preoccupied with pleasing God! I do not wish to *displease* God, nor do I wish militantly to *oppose* Him. Frankly, I am distinterested! In my particular way of life, to me and to the circle in which I live, and to the ambitions which I cherish, He is simply irrelevant. So far as God is concerned, I intend to maintain a passive neutrality!"

This, of course, is a sheer impossibility!

Created for a specific purpose, you cannot adopt an attitude of neutrality toward the God who made you, without being morally irresponsible. God is not optional, God is an imperative! For this reason, *faith* is not optional—faith is also an imperative! You either implement the purpose of your creation, by dependence upon God, or prostitute your humanity! "For whatsoever is not of faith is sin" (Romans 14:23).

The facts of the case are transparently clear: you were created to please God! Without faith it is impossible for you to please Him, so that without faith, whatever you do, no matter what it may be, is sin! The *only* alternative to faith is *sin*! That is why Satan will always present you with a reasonable alternative to faith, for he knows that if only he can get you to act in other than dependence upon God, you are defying your Creator, no matter how lofty your motives, or otherwise commendable your actions.

Of the One who came to be perfect Man we read, "For even Christ pleased not himself" (Romans 15:3). As *God,* the Lord Jesus Christ had the right to please Himself, but as *Man* He did not have that right. Whom then did He please?

He pleased the Father! "For I do always those things that please Him" (John 8:29).

So that at the end of thirty years, before Christ's baptism by John, and again during His public ministry, the Father could look down from heaven and say, "This is my beloved Son, in whom I am well pleased" (Matthew 3:17 and 17:5). To have acted other than in dependence upon the Father would have violated the perfection of His own humanity. That is why Satan's attacks upon the Son were designed to trick Him, somehow, into acting on His own initiative; but though tempted again and again, and *in all points* like as we are, He was without sin. He never once acted in other than dependence on the Father.

51

God is answerable to no one but to Himself, for He is the Omnipotent Creator. "O man, who art thou that repliest against God? Shall the thing formed say to him that formed it, Why hast thou made me thus?" (Romans 9:20). God's authority is final, and He obeys no one, for to obey would be less than an act of God. "Before me there was no God formed, neither shall there be after me. I, even I, am the Lord; and beside me there is no Saviour" (Isaiah 43:10 and 11).

Yet herein is the "foolishness" and the "weakness" of God (I Corinthians 1:25), that the Word, who was in the beginning with God and was God, and by whom all things were made (John 1:1 and 2), and "in whom are hid all the treasures of wisdom and knowledge . . . the head of all principality and power" (Colossians 2:3 and 10), should come into this world for your sake and mine, and do what as God He had never done! He learned to obey! He entered the school of obedience, for "though he were a Son, yet learned he obedience by the things which he suffered" (Hebrews 5:8).

Was it possible for God to be in the school of obedience?

Only if as God He was prepared to behave as Man! Had the Lord Jesus Christ on earth not only *been* God, but also *behaved* as God, not only would no one have seen Him, and not only would it have been impossible for Him to be tempted, but it would have been impossible for Him to obey. But because He was willing to *be God* and *behave as Man* at one and the same time, He was able to say, "For I have not spoken of myself; but the Father which sent me, He gave me a commandment what I should say, and what I should speak" (John 12:49). As the "Sent One," the Son placed Himself at the disposal of, and submitted Himself in total obedience to the "Sender," His Father, and "carried His obedience to the extreme of death, even the death of the cross!" (Philippians 2:8, *Amplified New Testament*). He was willing to "taste death for every man," (Hebrews 2:9) and suffer as Man for men what would otherwise have been impossible for Him to suffer as God *behaving* as God, for *God can never die.*

God, "the King eternal," is not only *invisible,* He is *immortal* (I Timothy 1:17)—"in the sense of exemption from every kind of death" (I Timothy 6:16, *Amplified New Testament*). But of the Lord Jesus Christ, the Son, it is written, "For both He Who sanctifies—making men holy—and those who are sanctified all have one [Father]. For this reason He is not ashamed to call them brethren, . . . Since, therefore, [these His] children share in flesh and blood—that is, in the physical nature of human beings—He [Himself] in a similar manner partook of the same [nature], that by [going through] death He might bring to nought and make of no effect him who had the power of death, that is, the devil" (Hebrews 2:11 and 14, *Amplified New Testament*).

In this amazing way our wonderful Redeemer, though never less than our Creator God, by His miraculous incarnation ". . . made Himself of no reputation, . . . and being found in fashion as a man, he humbled Himself, and became obedient unto death . . ." (Philippians 2:7 and 8), and says to you and to me now, "As my Father hath sent Me, so send I you" (John 20:21)— to learn to obey in the school of obedience, and to enter in to all the unspeakable privileges and blessings inherent in the *Mystery of Godliness.*

5

THE NATURE OF A MAN

And the very God of peace sanctify you wholly; and I pray God your whole spirit and soul and body be preserved blameless unto the coming of our Lord Jesus Christ (I Thessalonians 5:23).

It takes God to be a man, and godliness is the consequence of God's capacity to reproduce Himself in you!

In the light of these facts, it is necessary for us to examine the nature of man, discover how he has been made, and with what equipment he has been endowed which makes it *possibl*e for God to reproduce Himself in him. I am going to ask you to do a little "donkey-work" with me in exposing some of the basic facts of man's humanity.

If we are to place ourselves at God's disposal so that we may be used intelligently for the purpose for which we have been created, then we need to know something about ourselves. Sanctification is not a tight-lipped expression of piety dressed in black lace and a bonnet, so heavenly that it is of no earthly use—to be sanctified means that God is able to put us completely to our correct use, and only when this is the case are we truly sanctified.

For the sake of simplicity we are going to base our considerations upon the threefold description given to us by the Holy Spirit through the Apostle Paul in I Thessalonians 5:23, "And the very God of peace sanctify you wholly; and I pray God your whole spirit and soul and body be preserved blameless unto the coming of our Lord Jesus Christ."

Quite obviously, this description presents man as a trinity— "spirit and soul and body"—and this is called a "trichotomy." I am fully aware that there are many earnest folk who prefer to think of man as consisting only of two parts; a tangible part, the body, and an intangible part, the soul and the spirit lumped together as an indivisible entity. This is called a "dichotomy."

It will not be my purpose to engage in any kind of theological controversy, for in this, as in so many other similar matters, there is truth in both suppositions, as there is truth to both sides of a coin. No matter how it falls a nickel is worth a nickel, and you do not need to fight over which side is up—unless your game depends upon the toss!

To the fact that the body is tangible, and that both soul and spirit are intangible I readily agree, and in this sense I am a dichotomist; but that the Bible deliberately discerns between soul and spirit is to me equally indisputable, and in this sense I am a trichotomist!

> For the Word that God speaks is alive and full of power— making it active, operative, energizing and effective; it is sharper than any two edged sword, penetrating to the dividing line of the breath of life [soul] and [the immortal] spirit, and of joints and marrow [that is, of the deepest parts of our nature] exposing and sifting and analyzing and judging the very thoughts and purposes of the heart (Hebrews 4:12, *Amplified New Testament*).

The Bible declares that ". . . the life of the flesh is in the blood" (Leviticus 17:11). See also Genesis 9:4 and Deuteronomy 12:23. It is a physiological fact that the blood is manufactured in the marrow, and this "source of life," being of such paramount importance to the body as a whole, is buried and protected deep within the joints and the bones. The "joints" provide a unique "behavior mechanism," but it is ultimately from the "marrow" that there flows the life which *motivates the mechan-*

55

ism, and this in turn gives *expression* to the life which does the motivating!

This is a beautiful illustration given to us by the Holy Spirit! The joints and the marrow are interdependent if they are both to function properly, and the one is buried deep within the other. Together they form one entity, yet each remains distinct; they may not safely part company, but the one must not be mistaken for the other, and the final paradox is this, that the marrow itself lives only as there flows *through* it the very life that stems from it—the blood! ". . . for the blood is the life" (Deuteronomy 12:23)—not the marrow!

This is why the blood is sacred in the Bible. It represents the *very life of God Himself*—the Spirit of God *within* the human spirit, as the blood flowing through and from the marrow, imparting the very Life of God *to* the human spirit, from whence this Life must flow to activate the "joints" within the human soul, and produce that pattern of behavior which enables man to bear the image of the Invisible, and give expression to the Indwelling, Quickening, Motivating Life of God.

It takes *God* to be a *Man!*

I believe that you will find it of immense value and a source of great enlightenment to consider man as Paul describes him, "spirit and soul and body"—a complete trinity. Much that is otherwise confusing will become refreshingly clear, and large tracts of the Bible will become infinitely more meaningful.

The most important part of man is his spirit; that is why it comes first in Paul's description. The next important part of man is his soul, and the least, though not *unimportant* part of him, is his body.

In that the body is the most tangible part of our being, and that with which we are best acquainted (having spent many hours admiring it in the mirror), it will be simplest for us to begin with this the least important part of our humanity.

56

The body given by God to man is described in II Corinthians 5:1—"For we know that if our earthly house of this tabernacle were dissolved, we have a building of God, an house not made with hands, eternal in the heavens." This is your "earthly house," your temporary dwelling place, and you do not know how long as you are going to be "at home." One atom bomb and a whole lot of people are going to find themselves "homeless"—without a body—and you do not need to wait for a bomb if you would like to walk in front of a bus!

All forms of created life, however, have a "house to live in," vegetable, animal or man. Look out of the window, and you will see many forms of created life, all of which have bodies, and you recognize them individually and specifically by the particular *shapes* of their bodies.

In your mind you say to yourself, "That's a tree—it lives in a tree-house; and there's a boy—he lives in a hoy-house; but that's a dog—it lives in a dog-house!" You know a cow is not a carrot, and I would know *you* from a cat! We recognize each other individually as men by our own peculiar shapes—some more peculiar than others!

In common with all other forms of living creatures, we also possess that *physical* quality of life which enables us to grow and to reproduce. The tree in the garden was not always that size—nor were you! Some of us feel that our capacity to grow in certain directions is a privilege which we might acceptably be spared!

Our bodies, too, present us with a convenient means of inter-communication. The flowers invite their insect guests with exotic colors, scent and form, and a little nectar puts the final touch to their seductive art! No one could say that a nightingale fails to communicate, nor for that matter—a flea!

57

My busy fingers commit to paper what before too long your eyes will read, and should good fortune so dictate, maybe our paths one day will cross, and by the exercise of my thoracic and abdominal muscles I will cause the thoracic cavity of my chest to operate like a bellows, causing a draught of air to pass swiftly through my larynx and cause my vocal cords, all suitably controlled, to produce a series of vibrations in a multiplicity of wave-lengths to be conveyed in their own turn through the atmosphere; these will be caught by a cup-shaped appendage on the side of your head, called the ear, directed toward the outer ear-drum and conveyed by an intricate mechanism to the inner ear, there to stimulate the waiting nerve-ends which will dutifully communicate an impulse to a certain section of your brain, and you will know that I have said, "Good morning!"

I will have communicated!

Maybe we will shake hands on the strength of it, and add physical communication to verbal communication, but in any case our bodies will have come in quite handy as a means of expression!

There is, however, a marked difference between the animal and the vegetable kingdoms. A tree does not get aggravated by a lot of little weeds in the garden, nor frightened by a bull! That is one of the advantages of being a vegetable! At the same time, a tree does not fall in love with the young bush over the wall, nor laugh when a fat man falls through his deck chair! That is one of the *disadvantages* of being a vegetable!

In other words a vegetable does not *behave*! It has a body but no behavior mechanism which enables it to calculate, react or decide; this ability is peculiar to the animal kingdom and constitutes essentially the difference between an animal and a vegetable. The seat of all animal behavior is in the soul, and it is with this part of our humanity we must now concern ourselves.

58

That man is an animal goes without saying! We eat and drink the animal way; we breathe and breed and bleed—and die—the animal way! That man is not *only* animal will I trust become equally clear, but *animal* he is! Furthermore, as "fallen man," he is perfectly capable of behaving though *spiritually destitute,* and completely "alienated from the life of God" (Ephesians 4:18). His spiritual condition determines not *whether* he can behave, but only *how* he will behave.

Do animals, then, have souls? The answer to this question is found simply in the first chapters of Genesis.

"And to every beast of the earth, and to every fowl of the air, and to everything that creepeth upon the earth, wherein there is life, I have given every green herb for meat" (Genesis 1:30). "And the Lord God formed man of the dust of the ground, and breathed into his nostrils the breath of life; and man became a living soul" (Genesis 2:7).

The expression used in the first verse quoted above, "wherein there is life," as relating to "every beast of the earth, and to every fowl of the air, and to everything that creepeth upon the earth"—the animal kingdom— in contrast to "every green herb"—the vegetable kingdom—is an expression which corresponds precisely to that found in the second verse quoted from Genesis 2:7 and referring to man, ". . . and man became a living soul." Exactly the same Hebrew word is used in both cases, though differently translated in the King James Version, and translated differently again as "creature" in Genesis 1:20, 21 and 24; Genesis 2:19 and Genesis 9:10, 12, 15 and 16. In every case it is the same Hebrew word, and it means "soul" as applied to man or animal throughout the whole Bible.

The soul broadly speaking, is also a trinity—mind, emotion and will—and enables all forms of animal life to react mentally, emotionally and volitionally within the "capacity limits" with which each has been endowed by the Creator. A worm, for instance, is rather less intelligent than the average schoolboy, and certainly less affectionate, but it can still find its way around!

You *behave* by the exercise of your will under the influence of your mind and your emotions, and this process does not in itself require any visible activity on the part of the body. Your body is only required when you wish to give *outward* expression to your *inward* behavior—in other words, when you wish to communicate with your external circumstances, and the way in which you ultimately communicate by physical activity may far from represent your true *internal* behavior! "The words of his mouth were smoother than butter (*external behavior*), but war was in his heart (*internal behavior*): his words were softer than oil, yet were they drawn swords" (Psalm 55:21).

Do you get the point? You said to him, "You're welcome"—but in your heart you could have strangled him!

When last did *you* sit in church with the body neatly propped against the back of the seat, and with the gaze politely set in the preacher's direction, while all the time you were visiting with someone *fifty miles away*? How many heated verbal exchanges have *you* had with some absent foe whilst standing at the kitchen sink—and you never uttered a word!

What exciting moments you have had, and what frightening adventures—lying fast asleep upon your bed! Some of the best sermons I ever preached, I preached in bed! A pity only that on these rare occasions of unusual eloquence, it was the preacher himself who slept—and not the congregation!

Psychiatrists declare that far more damage can be done, and far deeper impressions be made upon the character by this "unseen behavior" of the soul, unmatched by physical action, than by the actual deeds themselves. The fascination of the cinema, in watching television, soaking in a novel or in scanning the many crime reports which fill the daily newspapers, is that the unsuspecting victim of this process "lives" the part of the chosen character in the innermost recesses of the mind and of the emotions, thereby satisfying some inward urge to be a "hero," attracting attention to himself, wreaking some awful vengeance upon unkind society, indulging some illicit lust, or fulfilling such ignoble ambitions in the secret of the soul, as might otherwise be incompatible, *if performed,* with the impression he would like to give to others of himself!

"The thoughts of the wicked are an abomination to the Lord" (Proverbs 15:26).

"For as he thinketh in his heart, so is he" (Proverbs 23:7).

"Whosoever hateth his brother is a murderer" (I John 3:15).

". . . whosoever looketh on a woman to lust after her hath committed adultery with her already in his heart" (Matthew 5:28).

Fortunately, this activity within the soul can be as beneficial as it can be damaging, nourishing nobility of character, and making such indelible impressions as may shape our future ends. Lofty deeds first cradled in the soul and later clothed with action in the light of day! It was with this in mind that Paul wrote to the Philippian Church:

> Finally, brethren, whatsoever things are true, whatsoever things are honest, whatsoever things are just, whatsoever things are pure, whatsoever things are lovely, whatsoever things are of good report; if there be any virtue, and if there be any praise, think on these things (Philippians 4:8).

Paul knew that to *"think on these things"* would inevitably provide the "dress-rehearsal" for their ultimate performance, profoundly affecting the behavior from within and from without.

The behavior process of the soul may be protracted and leisurely. On the other hand it can take place with amazing rapidity and be matched almost instantly with the appropriate physical action, as a driver in an emergency applies his brakes and swerves to a grinding halt, a fielder leaps to catch a ball and win the game, or some bodyguard throws himself in a split-second between his master and the deadly missile of his murderous assassin!

Supposing you became very angry with me, and highly excited—your *emotions* thus disturbed might well say to your *will,* "Hit him!"—and if your emotions dominated your will, what would you do? You would hit me! Probably, however, in the meantime, your *mind* —acting on information received through the eyes— would say to your will, "Don't do that! He's bigger than you are—and he will hit you back!" This is how you function thousands of times a day. You look at your watch, and the *mind* says to the *will,* "It's time to go!" and the *will* says to the *legs,* "Quick march!" and off you go!

Perhaps, however, your watch is slow! No matter, then, how sincere your mind may be in the conclusions drawn from the false information provided by the watch—you will be *sincerely wrong*! The train has gone!

Having believed what you heard about a certain person, your emotional reactions toward that individual may be adversely affected—and what you heard may well have been a wicked lie! Quite obviously, if your mental conclusions and your emotional attitudes are to be not only quite *sincere,* but *right,* they must derive from *truth*! Your morality may be determined by the degree to which your *will* responds to *right* mental conclusions and to *right* emotional reactions, and translates these influences into positive action. The basis therefore, of all true morality is *Truth*!

The Bible makes it abundantly clear that Truth is expressed through the Word.

In many separate revelations—each of which set forth a portion of the Truth—and in different ways God spoke of old to [our] forefathers in and by the prophets. [But] in the last of these days He has spoken to us in [the person of a] Son (Hebrews 1:1 and 2, *Amplified New Testament*).

Words are essentially a means of communicating information, and the information conveyed will affect the behavior of the recipient to the degree in which he acts upon it. When you *act* in strict obedience to the *Truth* revealed through the *Word,* the Truth *behaves,* and the end effect is *righteousness*!

As the Absolute Source of Truth revealed through the Word, God is the Absolute Source of Righteousness. Satan, on the other hand, as the absolute source of all that is *false*, is the absolute source of all *unrighteousness*! The first word he ever spoke to man was a lie, and he has been deceiving him ever since! He "masquerades as an angel of light" (II Corinthians 11:14, *Amplified New Testament*), and propagates his malicious lies through those of his dupes who "by good words and fair speeches deceive the hearts of the simple" (Romans 16:18).

It is interesting to note, that only man within the animal kingdom is capable of producing words and of recognizing them to any great extent in order to convey and to receive exact items of information; to hear, utter—or to distort—the Truth! Maybe his capacity for speech plays a far bigger part than we had thought in man's capacity to behave as a moral being. It lays him open to the Word!

Monkeys chatter in the trees and dogs may bark at cats, but though it may be very meaningful to them what they have to say is somewhat ungrammatical! Even if the parrot *can* say "Pretty Poll" or "Kiss me, darling," it has only learned to copy certain sounds—

no *message* is conveyed! What added complications would result for all mankind if once our poor, dumb friends could get together and discuss the stupidity and wickedness of men! What *lies* our Tabby Cat might tell the cat next door about the way we live at home! Let this then be our consolation—if these lesser creatures cannot *know* the Truth, neither can they very well distort it!

Notwithstanding this, neither animal nor man needs any particular relationship to God just simply to "behave." If you own a dog, when you get home does he not recognize you as his master, wag his tail, and run to meet you, indicating with his muddy paws all down your front how pleased he is to see you? The dog does not object when you enter the house through the front door; he knows you have the right, because you live there; but what if someone climbs through the bathroom window at three o'clock in the morning? The dog would think to himself, "My master doesn't *usually* come through the bathroom window at three in the morning—not often!" Then after suitable investigation, sufficient to satisfy himself that the shape of the body does not correspond with that of any friend of the family, as previously recorded in his memory, the faithful dog would discharge his responsibilities by indicating his distinct displeasure with the other, sharper end of his anatomy, probably to the detriment of the intruder's pants!

Take the dog for a walk, and when he strays too far you call him; then, standing in the distance, head on one side with one ear up and the other ear down, and with a mischievous grin on his face, the dog will hesitate! "What shall I do? Shall I obey?—or chase the cat? That would be far more interesting!" Then you shout a little louder, and with some impatience in your voice, and the dog remembers what happened last time that he disobeyed you—and it hurt! So he comes to heel,

64

tail half between his legs, and just far enough away from you to be safe!

All this behavior has in the first instance taken place within the soul of the dog, and the muddy paw-marks on your trousers indicate that on your arrival home, the dog has "functioned"; communicating to you his mental recognition and his emotional delight by translating them into volitional action, using his body to run through the dirtiest puddle he can find, and then jumping up to greet you!

I was staying on the east coast of New England some years ago, and my hostess explained the great dilemma in which she had found herself, in her desire to feed both birds and squirrels at one and the same time. She discovered that the squirrels had the unhappy knack of getting all that she provided for the birds, and she had used all her ingenuity to discover a means whereby she could segregate their appetites!

Then she hit on the master plan! From the second story of her home there was a laundry line which ran out over a pulley to a distant tree, over a lawn; and so, taking about two yards of fine thread and the lid of a tin to act as a small tray, she placed the peanut butter on the lid and suspended it from the clothesline with the thread, and pulled it out half-way between the house and the tree. That was for the birds, and no squirrel could get at that!

My hostess went on to explain that only a matter of minutes later, as she looked out of the window, she saw a squirrel run up the trunk of the tree, climb upside-down along the laundry line, hang by its hind legs over the tray, pull it up by the thread with its front paws, and eat the peanut butter! Then, dropping the tin lid, the squirrel returned by the same route to the tree with a big, satisfied grin on its face. That was not just *instinct*—as far as my hostess was concerned, it was not even *funny*! It was cold calculation, brilliantly executed, and still out-witted by the squirrels, this good lady has given up trying to feed the birds!

We may understand, therefore, that if all that we consist of is body and soul, then man is nothing more than a clever animal, and the natural man, in his "unregenerate" condition, behaves as if this were so. He busies himself primarily with "servicing" the body, and to this end goes out to work to earn his daily bread and such other luxuries as will add to the comfort or pleasurable use of his body; he is only vaguely aware that he has a soul, but somehow recognizes that he must "keep body and soul together," otherwise his kindly relatives will come and bury the body!

This is not irrelevant to the times in which we live, for although we may not discuss the matter within the compass of this book, the hypothesis that man is nothing more than the highest form of animal life as yet developed on this particular planet, lies at the very heart of Christless, godless and God-hating communism. This is the very basis upon which the theory of atheistic dialectic materialism is founded—a philosophy admirably suited to clothe that satanic attitude of arrogant self-sufficiency, which we saw in Chapter 4 to be the very essence of the attitude introduced by the devil into human experience at the Fall, repudiating both the indispensability of the Creator to the creature, and the moral responsibility of the creature to the Creator.

According to this supposition, not only does man cease to be morally responsible, but he has no eternal destiny; when he dies, he dies like a dog, forfeiting thereby only animal existence. Little wonder, therefore, that life on the other side of the Iron Curtain is held so cheap! We are threatened today on every side, from within and from without, by this wicked philosophy of human existence, and we need to know why it is that we consider ourselves to be *men* as *distinct* from mere animals, and not just *animals* that happen to be called men.

66

What is the essential difference between man as man, and the rest of the animal kingdom?

God has given to man what He has *not* given to any other form of created life—the human spirit; this though intrinsically indivisible *from* the human soul must not be mistaken *for* the human soul. As the marrow within the joints, so is the human spirit buried deep within the human soul, remaining essentially distinct, yet *together* forming that complete *immaterial entity* capable of endless survival after physical death, as opposed to the purely "animal soul" common to the rest of the animal kingdom, which possesses no such capacity either to survive or to be held morally responsible beyond the grave.

This capacity for endless survival beyond physical death must not be confused with "immortality," which is a characteristic, strictly speaking, of God alone.

> I give thee charge in the sight of God, who quickeneth all things ("preserveth alive all living things," *Amplified New Testament*) and before Christ Jesus, who before Pontius Pilate witnessed a good confession; . . . which in his times he shall show, who is the blessed and only Potentate, the King of kings and Lord of lords; who only hath immortality; ("In the sense of exemption from every form of death," *Amplified New Testament*) (I Timothy 6:13-16).

In God and God alone is life eternally inherent— eternally *pre*-existent, *self*-existent and self-*perpetuating* —and this characteristic of deity is shared equally by the Son, the Lord Jesus Christ, with the Father and with the "Eternal Spirit" (Hebrews 9:14)—"For even as the Father has life in Himself and is self-existent, so He has given to the Son to have life in Himself and be self-existent" (John 5:26, *Amplified New Testament*).

It is for this reason that God is absolute, self-sufficient and completely *independent*. All other forms of life, vegetable, animal, spiritual or angelic, are essentially "derived" and not "self-existent," and remain *dependent* upon the Creator as the One who is the only Source and the only Sustainer of all life.

> God that made the world and all things therein, seeing that he is the Lord of heaven and earth, dwelleth not in temples made with hands; neither is worshipped with men's hands, as though he needeth anything, seeing he giveth to all life, and breath, and all things: . . . For in him we live, and move, and have our being (Acts 17:24, 25 and 28).
> In whose hand is the soul of every living thing, and the breath of all mankind (Job 12:10).
> . . . and the God in whose hand thy breath is, and whose are all thy ways, hast thou not glorified (Daniel 5:23).

To quote the late Archdeacon T. C. Hammond, M.A., onetime Principal of Moore Theological College, Sydney, Australia (*In Understanding Be Men*): "Immortality does not merely mean endless 'survival,' but 'eternal life.' It is its *quality* which is important. Whilst the souls of the unregenerate will survive the disintegration of the body, only the regenerate can experience the life—which is of the same quality as the Divine Life—which has been 'brought to light' through the Gospel" (See II Timothy 1:10).

The human spirit is this unique capacity which God has given to man, which enables him both to receive and be motivated by the very Life of God Himself. To return to my illustration of Chapter 4, the human spirit is the lamp, incapable itself of producing light, but capable of receiving that which working in and through it produces light, and upon which it must be constantly dependent if it is to fulfill the purpose for which, as a lamp, it was created. "The spirit of man is the candle of the Lord, . . ." (Proverbs 20:27).

As translated in Proverbs 20:20, the word "candle" means lamp, and what the electricity is to an electric lamp, and what oil is to an oil lamp, the Holy Spirit is to the human spirit. With relentless consistency throughout the Scriptures, oil represents the person and office of the Holy Spirit, in whose person God is able to inhabit man's humanity and make him a partaker of His own Divine Nature, whereby man may be not only physically alive, as an animal, but spiritually alive, like God.

> For thus saith the high and lofty One that inhabiteth eternity, whose name is Holy; I dwell in the high and holy place, with him also that is of a contrite and humble spirit, to revive the spirit of the humble, and to revive the heart of the contrite ones (Isaiah 57:15).
> Whereby are given unto us exceeding great and precious promises: that by these ye might be partakers of the divine nature . . . (II Peter 1:4).

It is your capacity to receive God, and to enjoy God, and to be enjoyed *by* God which makes you man as opposed to mere animal, and it is only God in you that enables you to function as He intended you as man to function.

Lose God, and lose everything that truly makes you man and enables you to behave as God intended man to behave! The anarchy of godlessness begins! The human spirit destitute of the Holy Spirit leaves the soul abandoned as a ship without a rudder on a storm-tossed sea, spiritually bankrupt, dead—"alienated from the life of God" (Ephesians 4:18)—an easy prey to every evil, malicious and malevolent influence of which it may fall foul!

This has been the unhappy lot of man since Adam made his fateful choice! To rescue him God sent His Son—to make man *man* again! Man as God intended man to be!

"For I will not contend for ever, neither will I be angry always, for [were it not so] the spirit of man would faint and be consumed before Me, and My purpose in creating the souls of men would be frustrated" (Isaiah 57:16, *Amplified Old Testament*).

THE FIRST MAN ADAM

*And so it is written, The first man Adam was made a
living soul . . .* (I Corinthians 15:45).

Thank you for the "donkey-work" of the preceding
chapter, and I trust that you are still with me! We have
seen that when you act in strict obedience to the *Truth*,
the Truth *behaves,* and the result is *righteousness*—
". . . conformity to the divine will in thought, purpose
and action" (Romans 6:18, *Amplified New Testament*).
We have seen also that the Truth is communicated
through the Word, having its Absolute Source in God.
"Every good gift and every perfect boon is from above,
and comes down from the Father, who is the source of
all Light. In Him there is no variation nor the shadow
of change" (James 1:17, *Weymouth*).

We have seen also, as we considered the nature of
man, that the human spirit is that part of man created
to be inhabited by the Holy Spirit, that man might
exercise his will under the influence of a God-taught
mind and of God-controlled emotions, to the exclusion
of all other alien influences which would deflect him
from conformity to the divine will in thought, purpose
or action.

ADAM IN HIS INNOCENCY

In his innocency and before the Fall, the first man
Adam acted consistently under the gracious and exclusive influence of the Truth from *within* him, being
inhabited by God Himself. By partaking of and being
motivated by the Divine Nature, he was lifted out of

mere *animal* status and *animal* behavior into the noble vocation of *manhood* and *human* behavior—that of being altogether *god-like* because all his faculties were placed unreservedly at God's disposal.

To clarify the matter still further, allow me to draw your attention to the colored chart at the end of this book, and built up as illustrated in the following pages.

You will notice a line terminated with an X at each end, and five sets of three circles each, labeled A, B, C, D, and E. The line terminated with an X at each end represents the physical world in which we live, and the center set of three circles superimposed upon a cross and labeled C represents the Lord Jesus Christ in His perfect manhood. The other four sets of three circles labeled A, B, D and E represent man in four different relationships to God, as indicated by the key at the bottom right-hand corner of the chart.

As explained in the preceding chapter, man possesses a body in common with all other forms of living creatures and that physical quality of life which enables him to grow, reproduce and communicate, so that in each of the five sets of three circles, the circle on the line and containing the letter A, B, C, D, or E represents the physical body with which man makes contact with the physical world.

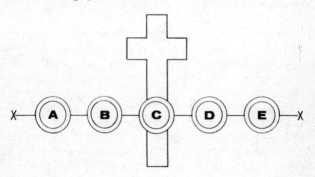

As opposed to the vegetable kingdom however, and in common with all other forms of animal life, we have seen that man possesses a soul—that behavior-mechanism which enables him to react mentally, emotionally and volitionally by the exercise of his mind, emotions and his will.

The soul is portrayed diagrammatically by the center circle in each of the five sets of three circles, four above the line and in the case of Figure B below the line. Basically each of these center circles is divided into three sections, representing mind (M), emotion (E) and will (W) as indicated by the key at the top right-hand corner of the chart and the center circle of Figure A on the chart. In Figures B, C, D and E the mind, emotion and will are designated only by the initials M, E and W.

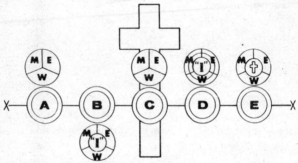

The presence of the capital "I" in the circles representing the soul in Figures B and D, and of the cross in the circle representing the soul in Figure E is explained more fully later in this and in succeeding chapters of the book.

In chapter 5 it has been clearly demonstrated that what distinguishes man from the animal kingdom, is that he possesses a human spirit—the "lamp of the Lord" (Proverbs 20:27)—this unique capacity which enables him both to receive and to be motivated by the very Life of God Himself. In the chart it is the third circle in each of the five sets of three which represents the human spirit; the highest of the three circles in each case except in that of Figure B, where it is the lowest.

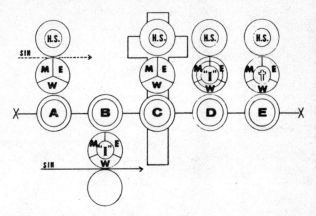

Thus by each set of three circles, extending either above the line as in Figures A, C, D and E, or below the line as in Figure B the whole man is represented—spirit, soul and body, as indicated by the key at the top left-hand corner of the chart.

Furthermore, on the main chart above the Figures A, B, C, D and E, God is represented in the Trinity of Deity by the larger circle sub-divided into three sections representing the Father (F), the Son (S) and the Holy Spirit (H.S.) whose presence is also indicated in the top circles of Figures A, C, D and E.

Figure A represents the first man, Adam, before the Fall, and I would like you to consider this with me for a moment, bearing in mind that to commit spiritual issues to paper in diagrammatic form must inevitably involve a certain amount of over-simplification.

You will notice in Figure A that the human spirit of the first man Adam is shown with a smaller circle within it, marked H.S. and representing the Holy Spirit, and though this in itself may be the first over-simplification I believe it to be legitimate, and I know of no better way of indicating the indisputable fact that God created man to be not only *physically*, but also *spiritually* alive.

When God gave to Adam the solemn warning: "for in the day that thou eatest thereof thou shalt surely die," it is quite obvious that He was not referring to physical death as the first consequence of sin, though this did become a *secondary* consequence. God was referring to spiritual death, and it is equally obvious that Adam was capable of *spiritual* death whilst remaining *physically* alive, a fact constantly asserted in the New Testament. To the redeemed Paul writes:

> but yield yourselves unto God, as those that are alive from the dead . . . (Romans 6:13).
> And you hath he quickened, who were dead in trespasses and sins (Ephesians 2:1).

for a Christian is literally a person who has been raised spiritually from the dead.

Apart from life however, death is meaningless! You can say of a piece of wood, "It's dead!", but not of a lump of clay. Clay has no capacity for life, and therefore cannot die—it cannot forfeit what it does not have; death is what is *left* when the life *that should be there* is absent! If Adam was capable of death whilst remaining physically alive, it can only mean that he possessed originally, in his innocency, a quality of life *other than physical*, which under certain circumstances he could forfeit, without forfeiting physical life.

What was the life which Adam forfeited? It was spiritual life—the very life of God Himself!

> In the beginning was the Word, and the Word was with God, and the Word was God.
> The same was in the beginning with God. All things were made by him . . . In him was life; and the life was the light of men (John 1:1-4).

74

When the Life went out, the Light went out!

When the Lord Jesus Christ raised Lazarus from the dead, how did He do it? He simply restored to his body the physical life which his body had forfeited, and without which his body could only rot. What happens when a sinner turns to Christ and his sins are forgiven? Paul says, "For as in Adam all die, even so in Christ shall all be made alive" (I Corinthians 15:22). Raised from the dead! "He made us alive together in fellowship and in union with Christ. He gave us the very life of Christ Himself, the same new life with which He quickened Him" (Ephesians 2:5, *Amplified New Testament*). Raised from the dead!

As the raising of Lazarus from the dead involved the restoration to him of the quality of life which he had forfeited—*physical life*—so it is reasonable to suppose that being *spiritually* raised from the dead involves the restoration to man of *that* quality of life which he forfeited by the Fall, *spiritual life*. The life restored in resurrection must be that life which *being forfeited* left behind the state of death from which the dead are raised!

How then is spiritual life restored to those who are redeemed? We know that it is by the presence of the Holy Spirit.

But when the goodness of God our Saviour and His love to man came to light, not in virtue of any righteous deeds which we had done, but in His own mercy, He saved us by means of the bath of regeneration and renewal by the Holy Spirit, which He poured out on us richly through Jesus Christ our Saviour (Titus 3:4-6, *Weymouth*).

. . . strengthened with might by his Spirit in the inner man (Ephesians 3:16).

Know ye not that ye are the temple of God, and that the Spirit of God dwelleth in you? (I Corinthians 3:16).

If therefore spiritual life is restored by the presence of the Holy Spirit, it is a reasonable supposition that spiritual death took place by the *forfeiture* of the

75

presence of the Holy Spirit. Furthermore, as already discussed in the first chapter, when here on earth, the Lord Jesus Christ did not play the part of *fallen* man, nor did He demonstrate only the role of *regenerate* man—He came simply to be *Man* as He as Creator had created him, with all the privileges and with all the limitations involved, and as *Man* He lived constantly by the Father through the Holy Spirit. Is it not safe to assume, therefore, that the first man Adam in his innocency enjoyed the Life of God through the Holy Spirit, even as the Lord Jesus as Man enjoyed the Life of the Father through the Holy Spirit, and as every redeemed sinner is *renewed* with the Life of God through the Holy Spirit?

I have taken time to consider this matter with you at some length, because in the absence of chapter and verse, you have the right to know by what process of reasoning the first man Adam, as represented in my Figure A, is shown as possessing the Holy Spirit within his human spirit. There may be others who would wish to explain the matter differently, and I will not quarrel with them so long as it is clearly recognized that Adam in his innocency was not only *physically*, but *spiritually* alive; that the spiritual life he possessed was the very Life of God Himself, not *inherent* in Adam, but *derived* from God and God-imparted; and that by the forfeiture of this Life, Adam was capable of suffering a spiritual death which physically, both in the area of his soul and of his body, he could survive. This will be the sense in which I speak of Adam being indwelt by the Holy Spirit before he sinned.

Referring again to Figure A, we see the human spirit of the first man Adam filled with the Life of God through the presence of the Holy Spirit; imagine now that this Life floods his soul—his "behavior mechanism"—so that his mind is totally, unreservedly placed at the disposal of the Holy Spirit, and his emotions are placed totally, unreservedly at the disposal of the Holy

76

Spirit. Who now controls his will? The Holy Spirit—the Spirit of Truth! Everything he does and every attitude he adopts will be an expression of the God who made him, who lives within him, and expresses Himself through him. He becomes the "out-shining of His glory" and the "express image of His Person"; God-like not by imitation, but by allowing God to behave through him.

Had we been given the opportunity at that time of watching Adam in action, we would have seen a perfect image of God, expressing *His* nature and *His* character, but God Himself would still have remained invisible. This image of God is represented in the diagram by the yellow margin at the circumference of the circle representing the body, for as we have already seen, it is by physical activity that expression is given to the behavior processes of the soul, making visible to the world without what is invisible within.

As God made him in his innocency, Adam's external behavior *in the body* corresponded completely to his internal behavior *in the soul,* which in turn reflected *exactly* the gracious activity of the Holy Spirit. He was a lamp that was lit, fulfilling the purpose for which God made him.

It is quite obvious that if this process had been purely mechanical, and Adam had possessed no capacity to exercise his own choice, he would have been no more than a robot; an impersonal "device," completely incapable of responding to or of satisfying the love of God, for only love can satisfy love, and love cannot be compelled! To win a person's friendship you clasp his hand—you do not clench your fist! All genuine affection springs from free volition, and you cannot truly love without the power to choose.

A little girl will love her china doll, because her imagination is vivid enough to imagine every kind of response; it answers back, it laughs and it cries—it can be spanked when it is naughty, and it can be kissed when it is good! But there comes a day when the old china doll lies neglected, staring glassy-eyed in the corner of the cupboard—jettisoned for the lifeless thing it is! Nothing now but the real thing—for all the calls a child may make upon her time and patience—can ever satisfy a mother's love; and the supreme prize? To be loved back! And God is love!

Man was made to love God back! . . . to reciprocate God's love to man. And Adam in his innocency, knowing that he had been created to please God and to bear His image, and knowing that he could only do so by maintaining an attitude of total dependence upon Him, expressed his love *to* God by total dependence *on* God! This was a faith-love relationship, which could not help but express itself in total obedience, for obedience is the only logical consequence of faith.

If you give me your advice and I depend on it, then I do as you say! This is the characteristic of faith as the word is used in the Bible; it involves an attitude toward God which always *does* what *He* says, and if you always *do* what He *says,* the world will see *Him* behaving through *you*—and that is godliness!

The picture then that we have of the first man Adam, before the image was marred, is of one whose love for God was demonstrated by his dependence on God, resulting in obedience *to* God. *Indwelt* by the Life of God, *controlled* by the Life of God, and *expressing* the Life of God! Spirit, soul and body wholly filled and flooded by God Himself.

When I view and consider Your heavens, the work of Your fingers, the moon and the stars which You have ordained and established; What is man, that You are mindful of him, and the son of [earthborn] man, that You care for him? Yet you have made him but little lower than God and heavenly beings, and You have crowned him with glory and honor. You made him to have dominion over the works of Your hands; You have put all things under his feet (Psalm 8:3-6, *Amplified Old Testament*).

Made by God to have dominion over all the works of His hands, man's authority was vested in him only by virtue of this "faith-love" relationship to God which would keep him always conformed to the divine will, in "purpose, thought and action," he was to be the visible means of communication between an invisible God and His visible creation, whose sovereignty "over all the works of His hands" would be subject only to the sovereignty of God Himself.

This was the significance of the forbidden fruit! It was at this point that Adam was to recognize the limits of his own authority, and maintain his attitude of humble dependence upon his Maker, knowing that his own "dominion" derived from God alone. Given the moral capacity to choose, it was necessary for man to have a point at which choice could be exercised, and by humbly submitting to this divine prohibition at the tree in the garden, Adam was able to affirm both his desire to please God, and at the same time to acknowledge that his very life *depended* on Him. In this way his love toward God found tangible expression in the obedience of faith, and qualified him to be the recipient of the divine Life, as the agent of the divine Will.

Adam had nothing to do to be alive spiritually—he *was alive!* God made him that way!

THE CONVERSION OF ADAM

Perhaps you did not know that Adam was converted! But he was, for conversion begins with a change of mind, and Adam changed his mind about God! He allowed the devil to poison his understanding, and believing a lie, *he died by faith!*

God had made it abundantly clear that the moment Adam repudiated his faith-love relationship toward Him, he would surely die, forfeiting the Life of God which makes man *Man*—for it takes God to be a man! Satan, as we saw in chapter 4, succeeded in persuading

Adam that he could lose God and lose nothing! That he could exercise dominion over all the works of God's hands without subjecting himself to the demands of God's will! He would now be his own free agent, enjoying liberty of action in the area of his mind, his emotion and his will, without the restrictive influence of the Spirit of God. He was to trade dependence for independence! He was to throw out his own big chest, stick out his own big chin, stand on his own big feet and demonstrate the adequacy of a man without God! He acted on what he believed from the lips of a liar—and died!

In figure A you will notice the introduction of the sin principle into human experience (the dotted arrow), "Wherefore, as by one man sin entered into the world, and death by sin; and so death passed upon all men, for that all have sinned" (Romans 5:12).

What happened? God had said, ". . . for in the day that thou eatest thereof thou shalt surely die" (Genesis 2:17). Did Adam die in the day that he ate thereof? Not physically! The next morning when he awoke the sky was still blue, the sun was still shining, and the birds were still singing in the trees! He could think with his mind, react with his emotions, and decide with his will; body and soul, he still functioned! Physically alive and soulishly active, the animal part of him survived, but the very day that he repudiated his dependence *on* God, Adam forfeited the presence *of* God! He was dead! Only the shell remained, henceforth to be a monstrous parody of the real thing (Figure B).

God had thrown the master-switch, and the Holy Spirit withdrew from the human spirit, and when the Life went out, the Light went out, and the soul of man was plunged into the abysmal darkness of a fallen humanity, uninhabited by God; and ever since Adam fell into sin every child born into this world has been born in the pattern of fallen man. ". . . by nature the children of wrath, even as others . . . Having the understanding darkened, being alienated from the life of God through the ignorance that is in them, because of the blindness of their heart" (Ephesians 2:3 and 4:18).

Godlessness, lifelessness and lightlessness were the inevitable consequences of Adam's conversion! Of his own free volition he stepped out of dependence into independence, out of life into death, and out of light into darkness! He was on his own! At least—he thought he was!

Figure B in the diagram shows the human spirit of fallen man (the lowest circle) now destitute of the Holy Spirit; sin has come between him and God. This in itself would have been bad enough; for in the absence of the motivating Life of God, in terms of his behavior, man would simply have been reduced to the status of a very clever animal, for remember, being spiritually alive does not determine *whether* a man can behave, but simply *how* he will behave—and even so, he might have been as harmless and as pleasant as a flock of sheep!

Something happened, however, even worse than the forfeiture of the presence of God! You will notice in Figure B, that a small circle has been introduced into the center circle representing the soul, and in the center of the smaller circle, a capital "I"! From now on man is to be "Ego-centric" instead of "Deo-centric!"—he has become an "I" specialist! And this principle of ego-centricity is called in the Bible "the flesh" (not to be confused with the human body) and has its origin and roots in the devil himself (Romans 7:18 and Romans 8:3). Another word used for this evil principle in the Bible is "sin," as opposed to "sins" (Romans 7:14 and 20; John 16:9) and yet again "the old man" (Romans 6:6; Ephesians 4:22 and Colossians 3:9), or "self" (II Corinthians 5:15).

In the absence of the Holy Spirit instructing and controlling his mind and his emotions and his will with Truth, Satan, who is the father of lies (John 8:44), invaded the soul of man, usurped the sovereignty of God, and introduced this evil agency to pollute, corrupt, abuse and misuse his soul and so to twist and bend his will that the behavior mechanism in man, designed by God to be the means whereby he should bear the divine image, was prostituted by the devil to become the means whereby man would bear the satanic image, for "He that committeth sin is of the devil . . ." (I John 3:8), or "takes his character from the evil one" (Amplified New Testament). His body became an instrument of *unrighteousness,* instead of being an instrument of righteousness. Thus man became infinitely worse than an animal, for emptied of his divine content, and his soul invaded by the flesh, the animal part of him became the plaything and the workshop of the devil himself. Yet in spite of this unpleasant fact, to which human behavior has given ample testimony all down the centuries, it is important to point out at this stage, that even in his unregenerate, fallen condition, man is still not just *mere animal,* for there is still within him—though empty of God and spiritually dead—his human spirit. This, added to his soul (as the marrow to the joints), not only enables man, though unredeemed, to survive physical death and remain morally responsible to God, but *before* physical death, makes it possible for a man to be spiritually regenerate by faith in Christ, no matter how degenerate he may have become.

To illustrate what I mean, supposing you were to hang potatoes from the ceiling of your sitting room in addition to the lamps already there! How much *less* light would you get from the potatoes than from your lamps, if you did not switch on the lamps! You would say, "No *less* light from the potatoes, for I would get no light from *any* of them, lamps or potatoes!" Exactly! Then why do you not use potatoes—if you get no less light from them; are they not cheaper than lamps? "Don't be so stupid!" you would say, "You can switch on a lamp, but you cannot switch on a potato!" Right

82

again! A potato cannot *receive* what it *takes* to produce a light!

That is the essential difference between "the animal man" ("L'Homme animal," I Corinthians 2:14, French translation) and mere animal. The unregenerate man "behaves" on the same principle that an animal "behaves," and as we have seen, because of the "flesh," far worse than an animal, for he produces the "works of the flesh" (Galatians 5:19-21 and Mark 7:20-23) but there remains within him the capacity to be "switched on again" by the ". . . washing of regeneration and renewing of the Holy Spirit" (Titus 3:5), and so to be restored to his true humanity, if he will repent and receive Christ as his Saviour; and ". . . if any man be in Christ, he is a new creature: old things are passed away: behold, all things are become new" (II Corinthians 5:17).

By his "conversion," therefore, the first man Adam not only lost the Life of God, and ceased to be in the image of God, but his whole personality became available to the devil, to be exploited by him, producing a race of men whose ungodly behavior, represented by the brown margin at the circumference of circle B, is a demonstration of ". . . the mystery of iniquity" (II Thessalonians 2:7), or "that hidden principle of rebellion against constituted authority (*Amplified New Testament*).

For God's [holy] wrath *and* indignation are revealed from heaven against all ungodliness and unrighteousness of men, who in their wickedness repress *and* hinder the truth *and* make it inoperative. For that which is known about God is evident to them *and* made plain in their inner consciousness, because God [Himself] has shown it to them. For ever since the creation of the world His invisible nature *and* attributes, that is, His eternal power and divinity have been made intelligible *and* clearly discernible in *and* through the things that have been made—His handiworks. So [men] are without excuse—altogether without any defense or justification. Because that when they knew and recognized Him as the

83

God, they did not honor *and* glorify Him as God, or give Him thanks. But instead they became futile and godless in their thinking—with vain imaginings, foolish reasoning and stupid speculations—and their senseless minds were darkened. Claiming to be wise, they became fools—professing to be smart, they made simpletons of themselves. And by them the glory and majesty *and* excellence of the immortal God was exchanged for *and* represented by images, resembling mortal man and birds and beasts and reptiles (Romans 1:18-23, *Amplified New Testament*).

In other words, man was no longer anchored to anything absolute, and so was at liberty to choose his own gods, as the objects of his own imitation, to suit his own convenience, to satisfy his own unholy lusts, and to feed his own incorrigible pride! "Because they exchanged the truth of God for a lie, and served the creature rather than the Creator, Who is blessed forever! . . ." (Romans 1:25, *Amplified New Testament*).

7

THE MYSTERY OF INIQUITY

For the mystery of iniquity doth already work (II Thessalonians 2:7).

When the Lord Jesus Christ turned to Peter and said, "Get thee behind me, Satan: thou art an offense to me: . . ." (Matthew 16:23). He meant exactly what He said—He was talking to the devil!

It was Peter who had *spoken,* but the Lord Jesus Christ knew perfectly well that it was Satan who was "behaving," borrowing Peter's humanity as a means of expressing his malicious and subtle attempt to dissuade Christ from going to the cross. Peter's reasoning was sincere, and his emotional concern for his Master genuine, but the conclusions which he drew and the attitude which he adopted were false, for neither stemmed from Truth!

The Lord Jesus Christ had already begun to show His disciples the Truth about His Messianic mission, "how that he must go unto Jerusalem, and suffer many things of the elders and chief priests and scribes, and be killed, and be raised again the third day" (Matthew 16:21), but Peter resisted the Truth unwittingly under the evil influence of the "flesh" (that sin-principle of satanic origin, always hostile to God and always opposed to Truth), and what to Peter was a noble sentiment, "God forbid, Lord! This must never happen to you!" (Matthew 16:22, *Amplified New Testament*), was recognized by Christ to be a wicked thrust from the devil himself, seeking to thwart the redemptive purpose of God.

The devil knew that Calvary would be not only the

place of his own defeat, but the place where man would be rescued from his clutches and restored to his true humanity!

Little wonder then, that the Lord Jesus continued, "You are in My way—an offense and a hindrance and a snare to Me; for you are minding what partakes not of the nature *and* quality of God, but of men (Matthew 16:23, *Amplified New Testament*), . . . of men, that is, "sold under sin" (Romans 7:14) ". . . For the story *and* message of the cross is sheer absurdity *and* folly to those who are perishing *and* on their way to perdition. . . . And we are setting these truths forth in words not taught by human wisdom but taught by the (Holy) Spirit, combining *and* interpreting spiritual truths with spiritual language [to those who possess the (Holy) Spirit]" (I Corinthians 1:18; 2:13, *Amplified New Testament*).

As godliness is the direct and exclusive consequence of God's activity, and God's capacity to reproduce *Himself* in you, so all ungodliness is the direct and exclusive consequence of Satan's activity, and of *his* capacity to reproduce *the devil* in you!

This is the "mystery of iniquity"! For iniquity is no more the consequence of your capacity to imitate the devil, than godliness is the consequence of your capacity to imitate God!

> For I know that nothing good dwells within me, that is, in my flesh. I can will what is right, but I cannot perform it.— I have the intention and urge to do what is right, but no power to carry it out: For I fail to practise the good deeds I desire to do, but the evil deeds that I do not desire to do are what I am [ever] doing. Now if I do what I do not desire to do, it is no longer I doing it—it is not myself that acts— but the sin [principle] which dwells within me [fixed and operating in my soul] (Romans 7:18-20, *Amplified New Testament*).

It is a frightening experience to discover what really happens when you commit sin! You cannot, however, begin to understand the mystery of godliness without beginning to understand the mystery of iniquity, because the principles involved are identical! When you act in obedience to the Truth, the Truth behaves, producing godliness; when you act in obedience to the lie, the lie behaves, producing iniquity!

The Lord Jesus Christ said, "I am ... the Truth" (John 14:6—all that He was, all that He did, and all that He said was *God* speaking; He was the THE WORD, and what He communicated was TRUTH—the Truth about God! To see Him was to see the Father. He was the Image of the Invisible because as Man He always obeyed the Spirit of Truth, and the Father *behaved* by the Spirit *through* the Son!

If you listen to what God has to say through the Son, you, too, will know the Truth, for He said, "If you abide in My Word—hold fast to My teachings *and* live in accordance with them—you are truly My disciples. And you will know the truth, and the truth will set you free" (John 8:31, 32, *Amplified New Testament*)—you will be godly! The Truth will behave, that is to say, the *Son* will behave by the Spirit *through you*, and "if the Son therefore shall make you free, ye shall be free indeed" (John 8:36)!

Consider now, however, what the Lord Jesus Christ had to say to the Pharisees, "Your father is the devil and you choose to carry out your father's desires. He was a murderer from the beginning, and is not rooted in the truth; there is no truth in him. When he tells a lie he is speaking his own language, for he is a liar and the father of lies. But I speak the truth and therefore you do not believe me" (John 8:44 and 45, *New English Bible*). In other words, as God is the Author of Truth so the devil is the author of deception; he is the *big lie!* Everything he is, everything he does and everything he says is *deceit!*

Imagine for one moment that I steal the uniform of a policeman, step out into the middle of a busy street and hold up my hand. What is the result? All the traffic stops! Although I am exercising a stolen authority, all the drivers obey me for the policeman they believe me to be. But what I am is a lie! They obey my signal— but what I *do* is a lie! All that I *am* and all that I *do* is *one big lie,* but the traffic still stops, and I control the behavior of every driver who does not know the truth! Everything I say as a bogus policeman will carry the weight of an authority I do not possess in them who are still in the dark about the truth, and who go on believing a lie!

This—precisely this—is the devil's business; and men are his merchandise! "For the god of this world has blinded the unbelievers' minds (that they should not discern the truth), preventing them from seeing the illuminating light of the Gospel of the glory of Christ, the Messiah, Who is the image *and* likeness of God" (II Corinthians 4:4, *Amplified New Testament*), and although there is no truth in him, and all that he is and says and does is a lie, so long as men walk in darkness and reject the Truth as it has been "embodied *and* personified" in Jesus Christ (Ephesians 4:21, *Amplified New Testament*), the devil will go on deceiving them, controlling their behavior and producing iniquity; they will continue to *do* what *he* says—and the big lie will continue to behave through them! " . . . and the lusts of your father ye will do" (John 8:44).

Iniquity is the inevitable consequence, no matter what you may be doing, if *what* you are doing is the result of acting in obedience to the big lie operating in the area of your soul, through the subtle agency of the "flesh." Peter was sublimely ignorant of this wicked process, and what he said was quite sincere, but his sincerity did not make it any less iniquitous! He was the mouth-piece of the devil, and what he said was loaded with mischief—and Christ rebuked the devil in the man!

You must be careful not to fall into the same trap! It

is pathetically possible to be engaged in all kinds of religious activity which is nothing less than Satan's subtle substitute for salvation; he will pose as "an angel of light" and he will appeal to your nobler sentiments, and his ministers also will "be transformed as the ministers of righteousness; whose end shall be according to their works. For such are false apostles, deceitful workers, transforming themselves into the apostles of Christ" (II Corinthians 11:14, 15 and 13); by "good words and fair speeches" they will "deceive the hearts of the simple" (Romans 16:18) and "with feigned words" they will "make merchandise of you" (II Peter 2:3).

If you are deceived in this way, the end result for you, as it was for the Jews, will be "a zeal of God, but not according to knowledge" (Romans 10:2), and that is to say—in ignorance!

What was the nature of their ignorance? They did not know the *Truth* about God's *Righteousness!* They had never entered into the mystery of godliness! They did not know that godliness is the consequence of God's activity in man, so that ". . . being ignorant of God's righteousness," they went about "to establish their own righteousness," and did not submit themselves "unto the righteousness of God" (Romans 10:3).

Of course, when you go about to establish your own righteousness, all you produce is "self-righteousness"— your own generous estimate of the measure in which you have conformed, by your own ability, to the object of your own imitation;—any credit which is due, of course, is due to you, and to you alone! You are to be congratulated!

Is God impressed?

Not every one that saith unto me, Lord, Lord, shall enter into the kingdom of heaven; but he that doeth the will of my Father which is in heaven. Many will say to me in that day, Lord, Lord, have we not prophesied in thy name? and in thy name have cast out devils? and in thy name done

many wonderful works? And then will I profess unto them,
I never knew you: depart from me, ye that work iniquity
(Matthew 7:21-23).

In the very name of God, and in the practice of
religion you can "work iniquity!" This is the mystery of
iniquity! It is a perpetuation of the Adamic response to
the wiles of the devil. The Fall of man began with an
act of unbelief; what Adam *did* when he disobeyed
God in the Garden, was the result of what he *did not
believe*, but what he *did not believe* was the result of
what he *did believe!*

He did *not* believe the Truth because he *did* believe
a lie, and the lie which he believed was that he could be
independent of God with impunity.

God had said, "Lose Me, and lose everything—you
will die!" and the devil said, "Lose God and lose
nothing—you will not die!" What God said was the
Truth, and what the devil said was a lie about the
Truth; *every* lie is a lie about the Truth. The Truth is
constant, it never changes; once you have told the
Truth, the whole Truth, and nothing but the Truth, you
have said everything there is to say; there is nothing
more to be said! There is absolutely no limit however,
to the variety of lies that can be told about the Truth,
but the Truth exposes every lie for the lie it is! There is
no neutrality in *this* war! What is not *Truth* is a *lie*
about the Truth, and is the *enemy* of Truth!

Adam believed the devil's lie about the Truth, and
had no alternative but to *reject* the Truth and *behave*
the lie! Because the *lie he believed* was that he could be
independent of God, the *lie he behaved* was an *act of
independence* of God—he ate of the forbidden fruit!
This was his *act of unbelief* in relation to the Truth,
perpetuated by an *attitude of unbelief* in relation to the
Truth—*an attitude of independence!* This attitude is
the very essence of "sin"—of what we have seen is
called in the Bible "the flesh," and from it stem all the

90

acts which we call "sins." *Sin* is the cause and *sins* are the effect; *sin* is the dirty well, *sins* are the dirty water!

> For from within, out of men's hearts, their evil purposes proceed—fornication, theft, murder, adultery, covetousness, wickedness, deceit, licentiousness, envy, slander, pride, reckless folly: all these wicked things come out from within and make a man unclean (Mark 7:21-23, *Weymouth*).

It is, however, possible to keep the dirty water inside the dirty well, but this does not make the well clean! Self-interest may produce a hundred-and-one good reasons for curbing the "acts" of the flesh without making one iota of difference to its "attitude"; it will remain as arrogant and proud and hostile to the Truth as ever before, whilst presenting a "virtuous front" to the world around, all "dandied up" with pious platitudes!

The flesh has an incredible capacity for self-deception, for it derives its nature from the "father of lies"; at one moment it will advertise its independence of God and hostility to the Truth by cursing and swearing, and the next moment will give a pious demonstration of its own self-righteousness by curbing this, its own wicked habit—like a man who stops beating his wife to show her how kind he is!

That is why God says that "The heart is deceitful above all things, and desperately wicked: who can know it?" (Jeremiah 17:9) and no matter how strenuously we may seek to be godly without letting God be the source of our godliness, ". . . we are all as an unclean thing, and all our righteousnesses are as filthy rags; and we all do fade as a leaf; and our iniquities, like the wind, have taken us away" (Isaiah 64:6).

Perhaps I can clarify the issues still further by the use of this simple illustration. Let the human spirit represent the Royal Residence, prepared by God for the Royal Resident, the Holy Spirit; imagine next that the soul represents the Music Room, and in it there is the Grand Piano of human personality—mind, emotion and will. The body, as the amplifier will communicate the music from the Music Room to the world around!

Do you get the picture? When God created Adam in his innocency, the Holy Spirit—as the Royal Resident imparting the Life of God—was at home in Adam's human spirit, the Royal Residence (top of circle, Figure A). He had unchallenged and exclusive access to Adam's soul, the Music Room (center circle, Figure A), and He alone had the right to sit, as it were, at the key-board of human personality, the Grand Piano.

Instructing the mind, controlling the emotions, and directing the will, the Spirit of Truth struck every chord in perfect harmony with the heart of God in heaven and a matchless melody rang out in evidence that God was reigning in the heart of man on earth!

God, however, had given to man the key to the Music Room—that is to say to his soul or heart—and this key was man's right to choose out of a free will. He would not outstay His welcome! The presence of the Royal Resident in the Royal Residence was to be a matter for mutual consent, for there was to be a "Faith-love" relationship between man and God. So long as the Music Room remained unlocked, offering to the Holy Spirit unchallenged and exclusive access to the key-board of human personality, God promised that the Royal Resident would remain within the Royal Residence—the Spirit of God within the human spirit—and man would share the very Life of God Himself, and declare Him to the world in which he lived.

At the same time, God made it very clear to man, that should the door be locked, and access to the Music Room be denied to the Royal Resident, He would not remain within the Royal Residence, and the human spirit would become destitute of the Holy Spirit. In that day, man would cease to share the Life of God; spiritually, he would die!

Man continued to enjoy unbroken fellowship with God, until one day the Deceiver came—the Arch-

Enemy of God and Destroyer of Man-soul, whose name was Lucifer, Son of the Morning (Isaiah 14:12). He had rebelled against The Truth, and had become The Lie, and the Father of Lies—for there was no more truth in him! More commonly he is known as the devil, or Satan, but cannot always be readily identified, for often he masquerades as an Angel of Light.

This deceiver persuaded the first man Adam that man could play the "Grand Piano" of human personality without God—and just as *well* as God! He pointed out the great advantages of being free from the restrictive presence of the Holy Spirit, whose absence, far from detracting from human experience, would undoubtedly enhance it, for man would then be able to pick and choose his own tunes; tunes that needed only to be in harmony with *himself*, and certainly not in harmony with God! Far from *losing* Life by losing God, man would *gain* life in an entirely new dimension—enjoying things which tasted even better than they looked, and which would make him wise—as wise as God! Indeed man would become his *own* god, and what could be better than that?

Suffice it to say that the first man Adam believed the lie, and locked the door of the Music Room, and the Royal Resident left the Royal Residence, which became strangely cold and empty, and although he could not quite explain it, Adam had a new and queer sensation which he had never known before; for the want of a better name he called it fear, and it has never left man since, and it still has the same strange effect on him that it had on Adam then! It always makes man want to hide, or run away! The funny thing is this—again and again he finds that what has made him run away from God has travelled with him! It is a *bad conscience*!

However, at least Adam was on his own now, and could have a crack at that Grand Piano! What he did *not* know, however, was that while he was talking to the Lie (that Deceiver called Satan) one of the Lie's sons (for he is the Father of Lies) *had slipped into the Music Room!*

Later, when Adam looked into the Music Room— there he was, sitting at the key-board thumping away at the notes, and producing the most excruciating noises, all out of harmony with each other and with everyone else! His name was The Flesh—and man has never been able to get him away from the Grand Piano since! At least, not on his own!

It was still the same Grand Piano, that is to say, the same human personality, but having once produced harmony, it now only produced discord! Adam started quarreling with Eve, and said it was all her fault; but she blamed the devil—and she wasn't far wrong! Then it spread to the children, and Cain murdered Abel— and the whole miserable story has been going on ever since!

No! This is not an extract from *Alice in Wonderland* —I have been telling you the story of *your* heart and mine! The Holy Spirit at the key-board is the source of all godliness; and the "flesh" at the key-board is the source of all iniquity!

You do not need a new *piano!* You need a new *Pianist!* That is what the Gospel is all about . . . how to get the wrong man *out,* and the Right Man *in*—and to exchange The Lie for The Truth!

On your own you cannot do it! But I have good news for you!

You can't! . . . *But He* can!

8

THE SECOND MAN—
THE LORD FROM HEAVEN

*... the last Adam was made a quickening spirit ...
the second man is the Lord from heaven* (I Corinthians 15:45 and 47).

The first man was Adam, and he died. The Last Adam was Christ, who came to raise the dead! The first man was of the earth, earthy; and the Second Man is the Lord from heaven! The first was the one who made the mess—and the Second was the One who came to clear it up!

In the preceding chapters I trust that you have come more fully to understand what happened when Adam fell, and what the inevitable consequences were for him and for the whole race of fallen men. Deprived of the Life of God, the "animal" part of man no longer bore the image of deity, for although "In the day that God created man, *in the likeness of God* made he him: ... Adam lived an hundred and thirty years, and begat a son *in his own likeness*" (Genesis 5:1 and 3, italics for emphasis only). Children were born, but not in the likeness of God (God-like); they were born in the likeness of their fallen forbear, to carry the marred image of behavior patterns dominated by the flesh throughout all generations.

Each child born into the world since the first man Adam died spiritually, and ceased to be true man—has been born "in Adam"; and the consequence of being born "in Adam" is threefold—if nothing happens to change it!

IN ADAM YOU ARE "ALIENATED FROM THE LIFE OF GOD" (Ephesians 4:18)

There is no exception to this rule, and it is not something that *will* happen, it is something that has *already* happened! As one who himself had forfeited the Life of God, it was utterly impossible for Adam by the physical process of reproduction to impart anything of the divine nature to his offspring; all born "in Adam," in all succeeding generations, have been born physically alive, soulishly active, but spiritually dead. "Dead in trespasses and sins . . . by nature the children of wrath" (Ephesians 2:1 and 3).

IN ADAM YOU "WALK AFTER THE FLESH" (Romans 8:1 and Ephesians 2:2 and 3)

There is no exception to this rule! "The Lord looked down from heaven upon the children of men, to see if there were any that did understand, and seek God. They are all gone aside, they are altogether become filthy: there is none that doeth good, no, not one" (Psalm 14:2 and 3, cited in Romans 3:10 and 11). Men are sinners not because they commit sins; men commit sins because by nature they are sinners: ". . . by one man's disobedience many were made sinners" (Romans 5:19), and you were born, as I was, with the *wrong* man at the "Grand Piano"! ". . . estranged from God; you were his enemies in heart and mind, and your deeds were evil" (Colossians 1:21, *New English Bible*).

IN ADAM YOU WILL "DIE IN YOUR SINS" (John 8:24)

This is the third and final consequence of being "in Adam" at the time of physical death; it means that if nothing happens to change the situation between your physical birth and your physical death, you will *die* in the condition in which you were *born*, spiritually dead; but your soul will survive to be held morally responsible to God for a wasted life, and to "pay the penalty *and* suffer the punishment of everlasting ruin (destruction and perdition) and [eternal exclusion and banishment] from the presence of the Lord and from the glory of His power" (II Thessalonians 1:9, *Amplified New Testament*); and there is certainly no exception to this rule!

Had God not intervened, there never could have been a *second Man* to walk this earth as God intended man to be; that is why the *virgin birth* of Jesus Christ is not a matter of secondary importance, it is *imperative!*

Had Jesus Christ been born as you and I were born, by natural conception, He too would have been "in Adam," spiritually dead, uninhabited by God, and dominated only by the flesh with its roots in the devil—condemned already to die physically as He had been born physically, cut off from God! As a sinner by nature, He would have been a sinner in practice; a fallen member of the fallen race of fallen men!

The Virgin Birth of Jesus Christ Pre-supposes the Utter Depravity of Man!

You cannot reject the virgin birth of Jesus Christ without repudiating His deity and His sinlessness—unless you are prepared to repudiate the Fall of man! For fallen man does not have what it takes to be sinless. He is spiritually bankrupt and without God; and it takes God to make a man godly!

To insist that Jesus Christ came into this world by natural birth and lived a sinless life, is to repudiate the Fall of man! It means that what was possible to Him as a *natural* Man, must be possible to you and to me as *natural* men, so that if we are not what He *was*, it is only because we do not *try hard enough!* If this were true, the message of the Gospel would simply be an exhortation to greater effort—an attempt to realize the inherent adequacy that is self-existent within every human being—including Christ! A message of spiritual regeneration would become patently superfluous, and the Fall of man a myth, for by nature man would have what it takes!

This in fact would mean that man can master his own "Grand Piano," and emancipate himself, conquering his own soul! Pardon me! but if I am not mistaken, I think I just saw the Big Lie smiling round the corner! Someone has just made him a Doctor of Divinity!

A theological student came to me not long ago and said that he had just had his first lecture on Luke's Gospel. The learned Professor had announced his subject as, "The Virgin Birth of Jesus Christ—*neither true nor necessary!*" To be as ignorant as that of the basic essentials of the Truth would be tragic enough in the simple minded, but to *expose* such ignorance in the name of *scholarship* to a class of students is *criminal negligence*, and a masterpiece of satanic genius of which only the devil himself could be capable!

To *accept* the Fall of man, and still insist upon the natural birth of Christ, is to number Him at once with sinful men, for "all have sinned, and come short of the glory of God" (Romans 3:23) and ". . . the scripture hath concluded all under sin" (Galatians 3:22). John is speaking of the whole race of man when he says in his epistle, "If we say that we have no sin, we deceive ourselves, and the truth is not in us. If we say that we have not sinned, we make him (*God*) a liar, and his word is not in us" (I John 1:8 and 9), and Christ would have been no exception to the rule of those who "in Adam," walk after the flesh, and who inevitably sin.

Robbed of His deity, and robbed of His sinlessness, what would be left of His work of redemption? His vicarious sufferings on the cross would be stripped of all validity, for He could only have suffered for His own sins, but never for the sins of others. His glorious act of atonement would be reduced to an empty, sentimental gesture; the tragic end of a noble idealist who drifted to disaster because He lived before His time. His resurrection would be totally unnecessary, and to avoid embarrassment must be explained away as the wishful thinking of some hysterical women, or the ingenious invention of some of His over-enthusiastic disciples!

Deny the virgin birth of Jesus Christ, and you have laid the axe to all the essential doctrines of the Bible; the Fall and depravity of man, the deity and sinlessness of Christ, the atoning efficacy of His death and resurrection, the necessity for spiritual regeneration as the basis for holiness of life, and the truth of the Bible itself! Little wonder that those who deny the virgin birth of Christ have little love for the Word of God; for the Truth exposes every lie for the lie it is, and every lie is a lie about the Truth!

The miraculous birth of Jesus Christ not only presupposes the total depravity of man,

It Furnishes the First Requirement for Man's Redemption—a Sinless Sacrifice

As descendants of the first Adam, *we* were born *uninhabited* by God—heirs of His absence—and inhabited only by sin. The Lord Jesus Christ, miraculously conceived by the Holy Spirit in the womb of Mary, was born *uninhabited* by sin and wholly inhabited by God! He was the Last Adam—the *second Man,* as sinless as He Himself had created man to be; He was able to turn to His disciples and say, ". . . the prince of this world (*the devil*) cometh, and hath nothing in me" (John 14:30).

Look again at the diagram at the end of this book and consider Figure C. This represents the Lord Jesus Christ as He was on earth; never *less* than *God,* but *always* completely *Man!* Who, though tempted in all points like as we are, was without sin, and though of all *other* men the Father could only say, "There is none righteous, no, not one" (Romans 3:10), of *this*, the Second Man, the Father could say, "This is my beloved Son, in whom I am well pleased" (Matthew 17:5) . . . the first requirement for man's redemption—a Sinless Sacrifice and Substitute.

> To wit, that God was in Christ, reconciling the world unto himself, not imputing their trespasses unto them; and hath committed unto us the word of reconciliation. For he that made him to be sin for us, who knew no sin; that we might be made the righteousness of God in him (II Corinthians 5:19 and 21).

How did the Lord Jesus Christ in His perfect Manhood present Himself to the Father? Through the Holy Spirit—represented by the smaller, green circle within the human spirit of Christ as Man, in Figure C. "How much more shall the blood of Christ, *who through the eternal Spirit* offered himself without spot to God, purge your conscience from dead works to serve the living God" (Hebrews 9:14, italics for emphasis only).

So that the Life of God, once clothed on earth with the humanity of the first man, Adam in his innocency (Figure A), and forfeited by the first man, Adam in his depravity (Figure B), is now clothed again on earth with the spotless Humanity of the Second Man, Christ— the Lord from heaven (Figure C), the Last Adam, the quickening Spirit—restoring the dead to life!

You will notice that in Figure C there is no smaller circle placed within the center circle representing the soul of the Lord Jesus Christ, for as Perfect Man He placed His total personality at the Father's disposal; the prince of this world, the devil, had nothing in Him. The result was that for the first time since Adam fell into sin, there was the perfect image of the Invisible God in bodily form on earth: ". . . the exact likeness of the unseen God. . . . For in Him the whole fulness of Deity

100

(the Godhead), continues to dwell in bodily form—giving complete expression of the divine nature" (Colossians 1:15 and 2:9, *Amplified New Testament*).

To indicate the unchanging Deity of Christ, even in His Humanity, the circle C, representing the body of Christ, is shaded yellow as are both His soul and His spirit. The complete expression of the divine nature in all His human behavior is indicated by the yellow margin at the circumference of circle C, as this once was true of the first man in his innocency, in circle A.

If God *withdrew* His Life from man when sin came in, under what circumstances will God *restore* His life to man? Only when sin has been cleansed and forgiven. The Lord Jesus said, "I have come that men may have life, and may have it in all its fulness" (John 10:10, *New English Bible*)—He did not come that men might have *physical* life—they had that; He came that men might have *spiritual* life—restoring the dead to life!

As the first requirement for man's redemption—a Sinless Sacrifice—the Lord Jesus gave Himself upon the cross and "suffered for sins, the just for the unjust, that he might bring us to God" (I Peter 3:18) and "the blood of Jesus Christ his Son cleanseth us from all sin" (I John 1:7), but it is essential that you should realize that His cross was the means *to* an end; for to confuse the means *for* the end is to rob the Lord Jesus of that for which He came.

He came that you might have *life! His* life—imparted to you by the renewing of the Holy Spirit on the grounds of redemption, to *re-inhabit* your spirit, to *re-conquer* your soul, so that you might be "transformed into [His very own] image in ever increasing splendor *and* from one degree of glory to another; [for this comes] from the Lord [Who is the] Spirit" (II Corinthians 3:18, *Amplified New Testament*). He came to restore to you all that makes the mystery of godliness an open secret—the presence of the Living God within a human soul!

101

This is the Way from death to Life!

When the Holy Spirit convicts you of the fact that you are a sinner, and spiritually dead—"in Adam" and at enmity with God—and you repent and turn to Christ, humbly accepting Him as your Saviour and welcoming Him back by His Holy Spirit to live within you, and to take control of you—this is your *conversion!*

In point of fact it is a re-conversion; as the first man Adam was once converted—changing his mind about God at the place of first choice, the Tree in the Garden—you, the heir by nature of his Adamic attitude of independence, change your mind *about his change of mind,* at the place of second choice, the Tree on the Hill,—the Cross!

Adam was created knowing the Truth from *within,* through the Spirit, and he listened to the Lie from *without,* through the word of Satan; and he exchanged the Truth of God for a Lie—The Truth went out, and the Lie came in! He stepped out of dependence into independence—out of Life into death! You were born blinded by the Lie from *within* through the flesh, and you listen to the Truth from *without* through the Word of God. When you *repent* you accept the Truth and obey it, stepping back out of independence into dependence—out of death into Life! "Verily, verily, I say unto you, He that heareth my word, and believeth on him that sent me, hath everlasting life, and shall not come into condemnation; but is passed from death unto life" (John 5:24).

The moment you repent and obey the Truth in genuine conversion, God accepts you for Christ's sake as a forgiven sinner, for "He bare our sins in his own body on the tree" (I Peter 2:24). Judgment has already been executed on your sin vicariously, in the Person of the Sinless Substitute, and you are acquitted, and this is called *redemption.*

Conversion is "man-to-Godward," and redemption is

"God-to-manward." God took the initiative through His incarnation in the virgin birth of Christ, in *providing* at Calvary the place where sinners may be reconciled to Himself through the atoning sacrifice of His sinless Son; but man must take the initiative in *appropriating* by faith this salvation which grace has provided. Grace provides, but faith appropriates, so that ". . . it is by grace that you have been saved through faith; and that not of yourselves. It is God's gift, and is not on the ground of merit" (Ephesians 2:8 and 9, *Weymouth*).

God bears witness to the faith which appropriates redemption by the gift of the Holy Spirit, and this renewing of the Holy Spirit is called *regeneration,* or *new birth.* "And God, who knows all hearts, gave His testimony in their favour by bestowing the Holy Spirit on them just as He did on us; and He made no difference between us and them, in that He cleansed their hearts by their faith" (Acts 15:8 and 9, *Weymouth*).

The gift of the Holy Spirit to those who believe is the end toward which the cross was but the *means;* redemption was never designed by God simply to make you fit for heaven—it was designed to clear the decks for spiritual regeneration, which would make you fit for *earth* on the way to heaven! You cannot be spiritually regenerate without first being redeemed, but you cannot be redeemed without becoming, in consequence, spiritually regenerate; it is the latter which adds validity to the former, and which is the seal of your faith.

And in Him you also, after listening to the word of the truth, the Gospel of your salvation—having believed in Him —were sealed with the promised Holy Spirit; that Spirit being a pledge and foretaste of our inheritance, in anticipation of its full redemption (Ephesians 1:13, *Weymouth*).

It had always been God's plan to "abolish death and bring immortality to light" by the "appearing of our Saviour Jesus Christ" (II Timothy 1:10) and speaking to "that old serpent, called the Devil, and Satan, which deceiveth the whole world" (Revelation 12:9), God had said, ". . . I will put enmity between thee and the woman, and between thy seed and her seed; it shall bruise thy head, and thou shalt bruise his heel" (Genesis 3:15). This "her Seed"—the Seed of the woman (Mary)—was the Seed promised by God to faithful Abraham, "And in thy seed shall all the nations of the earth be blessed" (Genesis 22:18).

Miraculously conceived and born at Bethlehem, the Second Man, the Lord from heaven,—CHRIST—"hath redeemed us from the curse of the law, being made a curse for us: for it is written, Cursed is every one that hangeth on a tree: That the blessing of Abraham might come on the Gentiles through Jesus Christ; that we might receive the promise of the Spirit through faith" (Galatians 3:13 and 14).

Thus the "promise" inherent in God's word to Abraham was the renewing of the Holy Spirit—spiritual regeneration—the raising of the dead! Just as the virgin birth of Jesus Christ furnishes the first requirement for man's redemption, so also

THE VIRGIN BIRTH OF JESUS CHRIST ESTABLISHES A PRECEDENT IN PROCEDURE FOR SPIRITUAL REGENERATION

What were the events which led up to the birth of Christ? How did it all begin, so far as Mary was concerned?

It began with the Word—a message of Truth faithfully delivered by the angel Gabriel, who "was sent from God" (Luke 1:26). The Truth which the angel communicated was at once strange and startling, contrary to all human experience, and beyond natural explanation, ". . . thou hast found favour with God. And, behold, thou shalt conceive in thy womb, and bring forth a son, and shalt call his name JESUS. He shall be great, and shall be called the Son of the Highest: ... of his kingdom there shall be no end" (Luke 1:30-33).

The natural reaction of the natural heart of this natural woman was one of incredulity! The obvious question to be asked and to be answered was "How?" And so Mary said to the angel, "How can this be, seeing that I have no husband?" (Luke 1:34, *Weymouth*); she deliberately denied the prerequisite for natural birth, and Joseph, too, denied any responsibility for parenthood!

> The circumstances of the birth of Christ were these. After his mother Mary was betrothed to Joseph, before they were united in marriage, she was found to be with child through the Holy Spirit. Now Joseph her husband, being a just man and unwilling publicly to disgrace her, determined to release her privately from the betrothal (Matthew 1:18 and 19, *Weymouth*).

The facts of the case then are quite clear; Mary denied intimacy with any man, and Joseph repudiated responsibility for the birth of Christ so emphatically, that he was about to break his engagement with Mary for her infidelity! Those who would have you reject the virgin birth of Christ therefore, would have you believe that He was the illegitimate child of a woman who was both unfaithful and a liar! Others would have you believe that a matter of such gravity is of no particular consequence! Remember that every lie, is a lie about the Truth—and every lie comes from the same source, the Big Lie, who is the father of lies!

> But as he was thinking this over, behold, an angel of the Lord appeared to him in a dream, saying, Joseph, descendant of David, do not be afraid to take Mary [as] your wife, for that which is conceived in her is of (from, out of) the Holy Spirit. She will bear a Son, and you shall call His name Jesus [in Hebrew means Savior], for He will save His people from their sins [that is, prevent their failing and missing the true end and scope of life, which is God] (Matthew 1:20 and 21, *Amplified New Testament*).

105

Joseph too, received the Word of Truth, and believed it; a message from God in confirmation of the prophecy of Isaiah (chapter 49:1) ". . . The Lord hath called me from the womb; from the bowels of my mother hath he made mention of my name." He was announced and named a boy, Jesus—*before He was born!* Maybe you have never thought of this—for we take so much for granted—but supposing Mary had had a baby girl!

"You ask 'How'—Mary" the angel might have said, "there is no human explanation! Yet I will *tell* you how—'The Holy Spirit will come upon you, and the power of the Most High will overshadow you (as a shining cloud); and so the holy (pure, sinless) Thing which shall be born of you, will be called the Son of God" (Luke 1:35, *Amplified New Testament*).

How was it to be?

By the Word of God, *through* the Holy Spirit!

All the mighty *power* of God to implement the *Word* of God, to clothe the *Life* of God with man's humanity was made available through the Holy Spirit; but was this enough? No! One condition still needed to be met! Mary's availability to this gracious, life-begetting ministry of the Holy Spirit!

Maybe you tend to take for granted the fact that Mary should place herself at God's disposal! Is there any reason why you should?—Have you placed *yourself* completely at God's disposal? Is there any reason why you should expect of her what you are not prepared to do yourself?

Mary might have said, "I do not want God to interfere in my life! I am engaged to be married, and I have my own plans! This is going to spoil everything!" Isn't this what *you* have often said or thought? In any case, who was going to believe her story?

Who *did* believe Mary's story? When the Pharisees said to the Lord Jesus Christ, "We are not illegitimate children *and* born of fornication; we have one Father, even God" (John 8:41, *Amplified New Testament*), it was a sly, stinging, wicked reference to the birth of the Saviour, by which these "snakes" and "brood of vipers" (Matthew 23:33, *New English Bible* and *Weymouth*) identified themselves with those godless theologians of all generations who have denied and still deny the virgin birth of Christ! Of these Christ would say today, as He said of the Pharisees then, "Ye are of your father, the devil" (John 8:44)!

In the light of events and in retrospect it is easy for us to call her blessed, but for Mary *then* it was the *deliberate obedience of faith;* by it she died to all her own plans, to all her own reputation and to all those hopes which had been fixed in the one whom she had lover most dearly! "And Mary said, Behold the handmaid of the Lord; be it unto me according to thy word" (Luke 1:38)—from that moment on the onus was on God to fulfill the promise He had made and to *do* what He had *said!*

By the Word of God, *through* the Holy Spirit *acting* on the obedience of faith! That is how the miracle took place, and Christ was born at Bethlehem—the Second Man, the Lord from heaven! Utter God and Perfect Man, by His incarnation the Lord Jesus Christ had established a precedent in procedure for spiritual regeneration.

The words of the Lord Jesus Christ to Nicodemus were as startling and as strange as those of the angel Gabriel to Mary! "Verily, verily, I say unto thee, Except a man be born again, he cannot see the kingdom of God" (John 3:3); and the natural reaction of the natural heart of this natural man to these unnatural words was one of equal incredulity! The obvious question to be asked and to be answered was "How?" And "Nicodemus saith unto him, How can a man be born when he is old? can he enter the second time into his mother's womb, and be born?" (John 3:4).

"You want to know 'How'—Nicodemus?" the Lord Jesus might have said. "There is no human explana-

107

tion! Yet I will *tell* you how—'The wind bloweth where it listeth, and thou hearest the sound thereof, but canst not tell whence it cometh, and whither it goeth: so is every one that is born of the Spirit,' (John 3:8). That is how, Nicodemus—by the Holy Spirit!"

By the Word of God (from the lips of Christ Himself!) and *through* the Holy Spirit!

By his very question, though one of the noblest of the Pharisees, Nicodemus exposed the fact that he only knew of one quality of life—that which he had received by his natural, animal birth, from his natural, animal parents; but "God is a Spirit: and they that worship him must worship him in spirit and in truth" (John 4:24). So the Lord Jesus Christ had to explain to him, "That which is born of the flesh is flesh" (John 3:6) and "flesh and blood" no more inherits the kingdom of God than "doth corruption inherit incorruption" (I Corinthians 15:50)!

"That which is born of the Spirit is spirit" (John 3:6) and if there is nothing "born of the Spirit" in that which is "born of the flesh," that which is "born of the flesh" is spiritually bankrupt! If you are still in this condition you need to be born-again, and all the mighty *power* of God to implement the *Word* of God, and so to clothe the *Life* of God with *You* has been made available through the Holy Spirit!

Is it enough, however, that the Holy Spirit is both able and willing to give to you "all things that pertain unto life and godliness," and to make you a partaker "of the divine nature" (II Peter 1:3 and 4)? No! You, too, must yield the obedience of faith! Changing *your* mind about *Adam's* change of mind about God, you must get back to God by a deliberate *act* of faith, as Adam lost Him by a deliberate *act of unbelief!*

You must look up into God's face, and say, "Maybe I do not fully understand how the death of Your dear Son, and the precious blood He shed can cleanse my heart from sin and clear the record—but this is what

108

you have said! Be it unto me according to Your Word! Maybe I do not fully understand how You can come by Your Holy Spirit to live in me, making me a partaker of the very Life of Jesus Christ Himself, so that He through me can reveal the Invisible God to a visible world, but this is what you have said! Be it unto me, O God!—be it unto me according to Your Word!"

Do that, and the onus is on God to keep the promise He has made, and to *do* what He has *said!* You *can't*—but He *can!*

Finally,

THE VIRGIN BIRTH OF JESUS CHRIST DEMONSTRATES THE PRINCIPLE OF AN IMPARTED LIFE

Joseph and Mary were accustomed each year to go to Jerusalem at the feast of the passover, and on one of these occasions, when the Lord Jesus Christ was just twelve years old, they were returning home, and "supposing Him to have been in the company, went a day's journey" (Luke 2:44), and having missed Him, they went back to Jerusalem, to find Him three days later in the temple ". . . sitting in the midst of the doctors, both hearing them and asking them questions" (verse 46).

When Joseph and Mary saw the "Little Lord Jesus" ". . . they were amazed, and His mother said to Him, 'Child, why have You treated us like this? Here Your father and I have been anxiously looking for You—distressed *and* tormented'" (verse 48, *Amplified New Testament*), and He asked them a very pointed question, "How is it that you had to look for Me?" (verse 49, *Amplified New Testament*). In other words, "Why did you *suppose* that I was in the company? Don't you know that I am wholly, exclusively available to My Father; that My whole Humanity is at *His* disposal, and I must always be about *His* business and doing the things that please Him? Why should you *suppose* that where *you* want to go is where *I* want to go? It all depends whether where *you* want to go is in My Father's interests."

By the miraculous birth of the Lord Jesus Christ, conceived of the Holy Spirit, the Father clothed Himself with the sinless humanity of the Son, in that body which He had "prepared" for Him in the womb of Mary (Hebrews 10:5), and the Son presented Himself without spot to the Father, so that He could say, ". . . the Father that dwelleth in me, He doeth the works" (John 14:10).

Through His obedience as the Second Man and the Last Adam, the Lord Jesus became a Life-giving Spirit (I Corinthians 15:45, *Amplified New Testament*), able to cleanse you from sin through His atoning death, and to restore you to Life by His indwelling Spirit, that He might live *in* and through *you*, as the Father lived *in* and *through* Him. Why then do you *"suppose"* that He is "in the company"—that where *you* want to go, and what *you* want to do is always where *He* wants to go, and what *He* wants to do! Don't you know that the Lord Jesus Christ lives in you *to be about His Father's business?* "And he went down with them, and came to Nazareth, and was subject unto them" (Luke 2:51).

Having established the principle quite clearly at this early age of twelve, both to Joseph and to Mary, that He was irrevocably committed to His Father, the amazing thing is that He then "was subject unto them." In other words, He would go where they went, and do what they did, but "His mother carefully treasured up all these incidents in her heart" (Luke 2:51, *Weymouth*) and she knew from then on, that wherever she asked Him to go, and whatever she asked Him to do, she first had to ask her own heart, "Am *I* committed to *Him* for all that to which *He* is committed to His Father?"

Are you committed to Christ without question and without complaint, for all that to which He in you is committed to the Father?

This is the principle of His imparted Life!

110

It involves complete, deliberate abandonment to Christ in everything.

"Do you not know that your body is the temple—the very sanctuary—of the Holy Spirit Who lives within you, Whom you have received [as a Gift] from God? You are not your own. You were bought for a price—purchased with a preciousness and paid for, made His own. So then, honor God and bring glory to Him in your body" (I Corinthians 6:19 and 20, *Amplified New Testament*).

There came a day, at the marriage feast in Cana of Galilee, when Mary learned to say, "Whatsoever he saith unto you, do it" (John 2:5); she had learned that *He* was not subject to *her*, but that *she* was subject to *Him*, and that was at the beginning of His public ministry!

When you have learned that *He* is not subject to *you*, but that *you* are subject to *Him*, that will be the beginning of His public ministry in you; you will "be renewed in the spirit of your mind—having a fresh mental and spiritual attitude"; and you will "put on the new nature (the regenerate self) created in God's image, (Godlike) in true righteousness and holiness" (Ephesians 4:23 and 24, *Amplified New Testament*), and the Second Man, the Lord from heaven, will reveal Himself again to a needy world through you!

The wrong man will be *out*—and the Right Man will be *in!*

9

THE LAW OF THE SPIRIT OF LIFE

For the law of the Spirit of life in Christ Jesus hath made me free from the law of sin and death (Romans 8:2).

The Spirit and Life are as inseparable as sin and death, and there can be no more compromise between the Spirit and sin than there is between Life and death; each is diametrically opposed to the other—that is why to be "in Christ" instead of "in Adam" involves a radical change of government! It introduces a new law!

It was to bring about this change of government and to introduce this new law, that the Second Man was born at Bethlehem, lived, died and rose again from the dead; "For as by one man's disobedience many were made sinners, so by the obedience of one shall many be made righteous" (Romans 5:19). The total availability of the Lord Jesus Christ to the Father—to be "about His business"—was such that ". . . after He had appeared in human form He abased *and* humbled Himself [still further] and carried His obedience to the extreme of death, even the death of [the] cross" (Philippians 2:8, *Amplified New Testament*), and as we have already seen obedience is the criterion of faith!

As the last Adam, the Lord Jesus Christ was the antithesis of the first Adam; *he* died by faith, because he obeyed the Lie; Christ *lived* by faith because He obeyed the Truth. That is to say, He was so subject to the "law of the Spirit of Life" that His total personality "declared" the Father.

No man has ever seen God at any time; the only unique Son, the only begotten God, Who is in the Bosom [that is, in the intimate presence] of the Father, He has declared him—He has revealed Him, brought Him out where He can be seen; He has interpreted Him, *and* He has made Him known (John 1:18, *Amplified New Testament*).

It is this law, however, operating "in Christ Jesus" which, the Apostle Paul writes, ". . . hath made me free from the law of sin and death" (Romans 8:2). How can a law which operated in *Him*, liberate *you* and *me*? This is the question which I want to explore with you in this chapter!

WHAT THE LAW COULD NOT DO (Romans 8:3)

Do not confuse the Law with the law of the Spirit of Life, nor with the law of sin and death. This is the Old Testament Law, and contained within it, of course, the Ten Commandments. It is the Law of Righteousness; what then could this Law *not* do?

The Law ". . . made nothing perfect" (Hebrews 7:19)—and the reason for this is now self-evident, for although the demands of the Law are strong and uncompromising, it is ". . . weakened by the flesh [that is, the entire nature of man without the Holy Spirit]" (Romans 8:3, *Amplified New Testament*). As one born uninhabited by God, and inhabited only by the "flesh," you discover that ". . . the mind of the flesh—with its carnal thoughts and purposes—is hostile to God; for it does not submit itself to God's law, indeed it cannot" (Romans 8:7, *Amplified New Testament*).

God, as it were, wrote the score, but the "wrong man at the Grand Piano" (Chapter 7) refuses to play the tune! He prefers the liberty of improvisation to the discipline of following the music, and the thrill of self-willed syncopation to the steady rhythm of a life in tune with God! Every departure from the score is a transgression of the Law and the transgression of the Law is sin! (I John 3:4) Has this not been your experience?

Written with the "finger of God" (Exodus 31:18), the Law represents the minimum demands of God's righteousness, and godliness will no more derive from your attempts to fulfill the Law, than from your attempts to imitate God—you can do neither! . . . for the law of sin and death within you is hostile both to God and to His Law of Righteousness, and so the Law ". . . made nothing perfect"!

It is a source of untold relief to discover that God has never expected anything of *you* but unremitting failure! Nothing that ever shocks you about yourself shocks Him; it *grieves* Him, but never shocks Him. You cannot be shocked by what you *expect!* If you are still shocked at your own capacity for wickedness, it is because you have never fully repented; you still do not believe what God says about you, that you are "unspiritual, sold to sin" and that in you, that is in your "lower self, nothing good has its home" (Romans 7:14 and 18, *Weymouth*).

You are still believing the devil's lie about the Truth, and rejecting God's Truth about the devil's lie. You are still committing the sin of Saul, who presumed to spare "the best" and "all that was good" in what God had totally condemned (I Samuel 15:9), and the folly of Jehoshaphat, who had false hopes of an unholy covenant, helped the "ungodly" and loved "them that hate the Lord" (II Chronicles 18:3 and 19:2).

You may be "in Christ," but you are behaving as though you were "in Adam," . . . perpetuating the Adamic creed of self-sufficiency, shocked when you *can't* only because you insist on believing that you *can!* You adopt the attitude of the defeated tennis player, who says there must be something wrong with his tennis racket!

I do not mean that God *excuses* your sin, or expects

114

you to go on sinning; I simply mean that He has absolutely no delusions whatever about *you* for what you are, apart from what He is! Why go on having delusions about yourself?

Repentance does not simply go on apologizing to God for the things you have done wrong, as though you were surprised at yourself; in that way you only advertise your own conceit! . . . as though you were waiting for God to say, "I know you did not *mean* it, and it is not what I would normally *expect* of you," when it is exactly what you *did* mean, and exactly what God *always* expects of you! Why not call your own bluff (and the devil's!) and recognize the "nature of the beast," for true repentance humbly admits not only that what you have done is wrong, but that what you have *done* is the inevitable consequence of what you *are*, unless what you *are* is replaced through the Holy Spirit, by what *He is!*

It is the Holy Spirit who is diametrically opposed to sin, and only His presence introduces the liberating law of Life. The "flesh" *loves* sin—and in all its most subtle forms, including "our righteousnesses," the "filthy rags" of pseudo-piety and self-advertisement (Isaiah 64:6). Stop being deceived into thinking that the "flesh" will ever change its nature; its roots are *always* in the devil! The late Captain Reginald Wallis used to say, "Far too many people have shares in the Old Adam Improvement Society. . ." It has been a bankrupt concern ever since the company was floated, and when the Lord comes, it will go into final liquidation!

The Law can no more make you godly than a railway guide can make a train run on time—and by nature you are always behind schedule! There is good news however; good news for you, no matter how discouraged you may be, for *"God has done what the Law could not do"* (Romans 8:3, *Amplified New Testament*).

How did He do it? He did it by "sending his own Son in a form like that of our own sinful nature, and as a sacrifice for sin, he has passed judgment against sin within that very nature, so that the commandment of the law may find fulfilment in us, whose conduct, no longer under the control of our lower nature, is directed by the Spirit" (Romans 8:3, *New English Bible*).

God passed judgment upon sin in your very nature in a twofold way; *morally* and *vicariously*.

He sent His Son in the first place, ". . . in a form like that of our own sinful nature" to condemn sin morally, and in the second place, He sent His Son ". . . as a sacrifice for sin," to condemn sin vicariously.

Though "in the likeness of," the Lord Jesus Christ was not *sinful as* "sinful flesh" (Romans 8:3, *Authorized*), for He was *without* sin, specifically *the only begotten* Son of God, conceived miraculously of the Holy Spirit in the womb of a virgin: "From the beginning He had the nature of God" (Philippians, 2:6, *Weymouth*). As opposed to the spiritually bankrupt stock of the first and fallen Adam, who being ". . . Ignorant of the righteousness provided by God" sought "to establish their own," the second and last Adam had the righteousness of God inherently in Him, "For the consummation of Law is Christ" (Romans 10:3 and 4, *Weymouth*).

Every demand made by the Law in righteousness found its complete fulfillment in the Person of the Lord Jesus Christ; there was no point at which the Law could accuse Him! In the beginning *with* God, and as its Author *as* God, Christ was the Law's *fulfillment* in righteousness; as Utter Man He satisfied His own demands as Utter God, and His Utterness was given utterance in Utter Righteousness! He was the WORD through Whom God SPEAKS and what He has to say at first condemns you!

It is quite obvious that the righteousness of Christ's

Life may be equated with the righteousness demanded by God's Law. This being so, what can the Life He lived *then*, nineteen hundred years ago, do for you *now*?

If the Life He lived *then* simply demonstrated the righteousness demanded by the Law, all that His Life *then* can do for you *now*, is what the *Law* can do for you *now*! . . . and we know what the Law *cannot* do; it cannot make you perfect! The Law condemns you, and proves you guilty!

> Now we know that what things soever the law saith, it saith to them who are under the law: that every mouth may be stopped, and all the world may become guilty before God. Therefore by the deeds of the law shall no flesh be justified in his sight: for by the law is the knowledge of sin (Romans 3:19 and 20).

His life also condemns you, and proves you guilty!

Compare your life with the demands which the Law makes upon you, and your mouth will be stopped, your sin exposed, and you will be proved guilty! Compare your life with the demands which Christ's Life makes upon you, and your mouth will be stopped, your sin exposed, and you will be proved guilty! Whether you try to fulfill the Law or imitate His Life, both will condemn you morally! By two equally absolute standards of measurement, you will be exposed for the sinner you are, for you have ". . . come short of the glory of God" (Romans 3:23).

The plumb-line may show me that the wall in my garden is crooked, but it will not put it straight, and had Jesus Christ come into this world simply to demonstrate a sinless life, and leave us with a matchless example, He would have left us to wallow in the squalor of our own inadequacy; the "good news" of the Gospel would have been a message of despair—to mock us, without being able to mend us!

117

The Life He lived on earth condemns you—for He *could* . . . but you *can't!* Then why did He live *then* a Life that can only condemn you *now?* Because

THE LIFE HE LIVED QUALIFIED HIM FOR THE DEATH HE DIED

The Lord Jesus Christ could not have died the death He died, had He not lived the life He lived! He could have suffered a martyr's death, a prophet's death, a preacher's death—the death of a noble idealist, the champion of some lofty cause, or as the hero of some courageous enterprise destined to bless mankind, but *not a Saviour's death!* "For Christ, the Messiah, [Himself] died for sins once for all, the Righteous for the unrighteous—the Just for the unjust, the Innocent for the guilty—that He might bring us to God" (I Peter 3:18, *Amplified New Testament*).

> Because the sinless Saviour died,
> My sinful soul is counted free;
> And God the Just is satisfied,
> To look on Him, and pardon me!

God sent His Son into the world not only ". . . in a form like that of our own sinful nature" to condemn sin *morally*, but ". . . as a sacrifice for sin," to condemn sin *vicariously*.

"For he hath made him to be sin for us, who knew no sin; that we might be made the righteousness of God in him" (II Corinthians 5:21).

The Bible leaves us in absolutely no doubt about the significance of the death of Christ; He died in your place and mine, incurring for our sakes a penalty that He did not deserve. This was no sentimental gesture, but a deliberate act of redemption! Apart from His death, His life could only condemn us, like the Law which His life fulfilled; but His death added *grace to truth*

118

G . . . God's
R . . . Riches
A . . . At
C . . . Christ's
E . . . Expense

Truth declared by the Law and fulfilled by His life convicts sinners of their sins, and tells them to be sorry; but *grace* provided by His death tells sinners who are sorry how they may be saved! "For the law was given by Moses, but grace and truth came by Jesus Christ" (John 1:17).

Without a sinless life, the Lord Jesus Christ could never have suffered a vicarious, substitutionary and atoning death. To deny the supernatural nature of His birth is to deny His deity; to deny His deity is to deny His sinlessness, and to deny His sinlessness is to deny the atonement; and to deny *that*, is to deny that God has *done* what the Law could not *do!*

Have you accepted Christ as your Redeemer? Do you know that for His dear sake your sins are forgiven? You may know this just as soon as you say, "Thank You, Lord! Be it unto me according to Your Word! Redeem my soul, cleanse my heart, and wash me in the Blood of the Lamb; the Lamb of God that taketh away the sin of the world!"

> In peace let me resign my breath,
> And Thy salvation see;
> My sins deserve eternal death,
> But *Jesus* died for me!

To know your sins are gone is joy indeed! The record cleansed, and reconciled to God, heaven is now your home; but is that really all you need?

It is where you must *begin*, but it is not all you need!

Does the knowledge that your sins have been forgiven, *in itself*, impart to you any new capacity to live a

119

different kind of life? The answer obviously is—No!

There may have been created within you a genuine desire to serve God, out of a sincere sense of gratitude to Christ for dying for you; you may be impelled out of a sense of duty as a Christian, to seek conformity to some pattern of behavior which has been imposed upon you as the norm for Christian living; you may be deeply moved by the need of others all around you, and holy ambitions may have been stirred within your heart, to count for God; if however, all that has happened is that your sins have been forgiven, because you have accepted Christ as the Saviour who died for you, leaving you *since* your conversion only with those resources which you had *before* your conversion, then you will have no alternative but to "Christianize" the "flesh" and try to teach it to "behave" in such a way that it will be godly!

That is a sheer impossibility!

The nature of the "flesh" never changes, no matter how you may coerce it or conform it; it is rotten through and through, even with a Bible under its arm, a check for missions in its hand, and an evangelical look on its face! You need something more than forgiveness, and *what* you need is the *big news* of the Gospel! This is the very heart of the message, for if the life that Christ lived, qualified Him for the death that He died, then

The Death That He Died Qualified You for the Life That He Lived!

The moment you are redeemed through the atoning death of Christ upon the cross, (see diagram) you receive the Holy Spirit within your human spirit, represented by the small green circle in the top circle of Figure D. You have "passed from death to life"—raised from the dead—and the Life which has been imparted to you by the Holy Spirit is the very Life of

Christ Himself; ". . . He made us alive together in fellowship and in union with Christ.—He gave us the very life of Christ Himself, the same new life with which He quickened Him" (Ephesians 2:5, *Amplified New Testament*).

The life that the Lord Jesus Christ lived *for* you nineteen hundred years ago—condemns you; but the life that He now lives *in* you—saves you! The Christian life is the Life which He lived *then*, lived *now* by Him *in* you. As He behaved in the sinless Humanity which the Father had prepared for Him then, so He wants to behave in your humanity presented to Him now.

Your mind placed at His disposal through the indwelling Holy Spirit; your emotions, your will, all that you are and have, made available to the Lord Jesus Christ as a living member of His new corporate body on earth, which is called the church.

This is the new law in action, the law of the Spirit of Life in Christ Jesus, re-establishing the "faith-love" relationship between your soul and God, making it possible for you to "declare" the Son, as once the Son "declared" the Father. Your "behavior mechanism" once more wholly "Deo-centric" instead of "Ego-centric." ". . . so that the commandment of the law may find fulfillment" in you, whose conduct, no longer under the control of your lower nature, "is directed by the Spirit." A radical change of government!

We see then certain principles evolving, and I would like to summarize them in four simple sentences:

1. HE HAD TO COME AS HE DID (miraculous birth)
   TO BE WHAT HE WAS (perfect)
2. HE HAD TO BE WHAT HE WAS (perfect)
   TO DO WHAT HE DID (redeem).
3. HE HAD TO DO WHAT HE DID (redeem)
   THAT YOU MIGHT HAVE WHAT HE IS (life).
4. YOU MUST HAVE WHAT HE IS (life)
   TO BE WHAT HE WAS (perfect)

HE HAD TO COME AS HE DID (miraculous birth)
TO BE WHAT HE WAS (perfect)

His supernatural birth qualified Him for the sinless life He lived, the Word Incarnate, never less than God in what He *was*, but never more than Man in what He *did!* Completely empty of sin, always *filled* with the Spirit, and *led* by the Spirit and *empowered* by the Spirit (Luke 4:1 and 14).

Could He not have chosen His own path and made His own decisions? As God, Yes!—As Man, No! Did He have no power of His own? As God, enough to create the universes, to throw them into space, and keep them there "by the word of His power"!—As Man, none! "Then answered Jesus and said unto them, Verily, verily, I say unto you, The Son can do nothing of himself, but what he seeth the Father do: for what things soever he doeth, these also doeth the Son likewise" (John 5:19).

HE HAD TO BE WHAT HE WAS (perfect)
TO DO WHAT HE DID (redeem)

Only by virtue of His own sinlessness could He die *vicariously* for those whose sin His life had condemned *morally*. God has done what the Law could not do!

> He knew how wicked man had been,
> He knew that God must punish sin;
> So out of pity Jesus said:
> I'll bear the punishment instead!

HE HAD TO DO WHAT HE DID (redeem)
THAT YOU MIGHT HAVE WHAT HE IS (life)

Here is the "much more" of your salvation! Christ in the present tense! Not what He was—that would condemn you; and not just what He will be—that would only tantalize you, but all the overwhelming adequacy of all that He *is right now*, for every step of the way, and for every bend in the road! "For if, when we were enemies, we were reconciled to God by the death of his Son, much more, being reconciled, we shall be saved by his life" (Romans 5:10).

You Must Have What He Is (life) To Be What He Was (perfect)

For godliness is not the consequence of your capacity to imitate God, but the consequence of His capacity to reproduce Himself in you; not self-righteousness, but Christ-righteousness; the righteousness which is by faith—a faith which by renewed dependence upon God releases His divine action, to restore the marred image of the Invisible God. It is not inactivity, but Christ-activity; God in action accomplishing the divine end through human personality—never reducing man to the status of a cabbage, but exalting man to the stature of a king! "For if by one man's offence death reigned by one; much more they which receive abundance of grace and of the gift of righteousness shall reign in life by one, Jesus Christ" (Romans 5:17).

At first sight this might seem to offer to you the possibility of sinless perfection as the result of spiritual regeneration, but this is far from being the case; for it is only your faith and your obedience which allow Him to be in you *now* what He was *then* (perfect)—and you will be what He was *then* only to the degree in which you allow Him to be in you what He is *now* (perfect)!

All of the Father was available to all of the Son, because by His faith-love relationship, all of the Son was available to all of the Father, and this constituted His perfect manhood; and the availability of the Son to you will be in the degree of your availability to the Son, because of *your* faith-love relationship to Him!

123

Had you *perfect* faith and *perfect* love, you could enjoy His *perfect* life—but these you do not have; for although you have been restored to life by the presence of the Holy Spirit within your human spirit, there is no eradication of the "flesh," which as you will see represented in Figure D by the smaller, inner circle containing the Capital I, is still operative within the human soul. The "wrong man" still clings tenaciously to his seat at the keyboard of the "Grand Piano," and resists every attempt on the part of the "Right Man" to take over!

This is the problem of the "carnal Christian," who although indwelt by the Holy Spirit is still dominated to a large degree by the "flesh"; the image of the Invisible God is only partially restored, as indicated by the marginal ring around circle D, half brown—representing still the "works of the flesh," and half yellow—representing the "fruits of the Spirit." Only in certain areas of the carnal Christian's life, and to a limited degree, is the Lord Jesus allowed to "be Himself" and to *express* Himself through the "behavior mechanism" of the believer placed only spasmodically at His disposal.

In other words, though you may be redeemed and regenerate, God never deprives you of your moral capacity to choose. The *act* of changing your mind about Adam's change of mind, which constituted your conversion, and which brought about your reconciliation to God through faith in Christ, must be followed by an *attitude* which perpetuates the change of mind, if you are to enter experientially into all the good of the New Life in Christ, of whose divine nature you have become a partaker (II Peter 1:4).

If the initial *act* of faith was genuine by which you were redeemed (and you will only *be* redeemed if the initial act of faith *was* genuine) your subsequent *attitude* will never change the consequences of the *act*—

you will remain redeemed by His "one sacrifice for sins for ever" (Hebrews 10:12) and irrevocably "sealed with that Holy Spirit of promise" (Ephesians 1:13), by whom God ". . . [has also appropriated and acknowledged us as His], putting His seal upon us and giving us His (Holy) Spirit in our hearts as the security deposit *and* guarantee [of the fulfillment of His promise]" (II Corinthians 1:22, *Amplified New Testament*); but your subsequent attitude *will* determine *on the way to heaven*, how far it will be possible for the Lord Jesus Christ to implement in you that for which He has redeemed you!

It is your inherent right to choose, which enables you to enter into this unique relationship with Christ—or to reject Him; but you reject Him at your peril! It has been magnificently demonstrated in the film, "City of the Bees," produced by the Moody Bible Institute of Science, that there is an instinctive interlock between this tiny insect and its behavior patterns, as in the case of every other form of animal life, only man excepted; upon the efficiency of this interlock its very existence and survival depend. Remove the interlock, and order would be swallowed up in chaos; the social logistic, structural and administrative problems of a bee society would be way and beyond the mental capacity of the most progressive individual bee! Anarchy would inevitably precede disaster and extinction!

No such interlock exists between man and *his* behavior patterns, for God created man to be a moral being, to enter into all the hidden depths of this amazing mystery—the mystery of godliness! The only interlock, the interlock of faith and love to God, allowing *Him* to reproduce *Himself* in man; and make man *man* after the immaculate image of his Maker!

Remove *this* interlock, and little wonder that across the rubble of a wrecked society of men, a lonely cross has cast its shadow; the shadow of a lonely God, waiting for men to be made *men* again, as God intended men to be; and it takes God to be a *Man!*

That is why it takes Christ to be a Christian—for Christ in a Christian puts God back into the man!

10

HOW MUCH ARE YOU WORTH?

And that he died for all, that they which live should not henceforth live unto themselves, but unto him which died for them, and rose again (II Corinthians 5:15).

Christ died to kill death dead, and to swallow it up in victory! He drew its sting—for "The sting of death is sin" (I Corinthians 15:56), and ". . . he appeared to put away sin by the sacrifice of himself" (Hebrews 9:26). This He did for all men, without exception, ". . . not willing that any should perish, but that all should come to repentance" (II Peter 3:9).

Never allow anyone to deceive you into believing that God has placed an arbitrary limitation upon the efficacy of the blood of Christ, or that there are those who cannot repent, even if they would, simply because God has deliberately placed them outside the scope of His redemptive purpose! This blasphemes the grace, the love and the integrity of God, and makes Him morally responsible for the unbelief of the unbeliever, for the impenitence of the impenitent, and saddles Him squarely with the guilt of the guilty—as an aider and abettor of their sin!

Such is not the teaching of the Bible, for the Lord Jesus Christ made it abundantly clear that the reluctance is on *man's* part, not on God's!

"O Jerusalem, Jerusalem, the city that murders the prophets and stones the messengers sent to her! How often have I longed to gather your children, as a hen gathers her brood under her wings, but you would not let me" (Luke 13:34, *New English Bible*).

It is equally clear from the Saviour's lips, that the wrath of God abides on those who do not believe, and that these will not see Life, for ". . . this is the condemnation, that light is come into the world, and men loved darkness rather than light, because their deeds were evil" (John 3:19); and whether men love Light or love darkness, God or the devil, heaven or hell, love can only be expressed by the exercise of a free will.

Without freedom of choice it is equally impossible to obey or to disobey—to be commended for the one or to be condemned for the other! I cannot blame my typewriter for the spelling mistakes it makes, nor congratulate it for its beautiful prose—it is an impersonal machine! It neither offers its services, nor withholds them, for it has no capacity to choose; yet it is precisely at this point that men are held morally responsible to God, who will take vengeance ". . . on them that know not God, and that obey not the Gospel of our Lord Jesus Christ: who shall be punished with everlasting destruction from the presence of the Lord, and from the glory of his power" (II Thessalonians 1:8 and 9).

Some would have you believe that only those can obey the Gospel and accept Christ as their Saviour, to whom God has given the ability to obey as a purely arbitrary, mechanical act on His part, leaving no option in the matter to any individual either way! On the basis of this strange hypothesis, the fearful judgment of God is to fall upon those who have remained in their rebellious state of unbelief, only because they have been unable to exercise an ability to obey the Gospel, which only God can give, and which He has refused to give them! Needless to say, such an idea can only serve to bring the righteousness and judgment of God into contempt and disrepute.

The revelation that God has given to us by His Holy Spirit through the apostles is delightfully clear: ". . . if any man sin, we have an advocate with the Father, Jesus Christ the righteous: And He is the propitiation for our sins: and not for ours only, but also for the sins of the whole world" (I John 2:2); ". . . Who gave himself a ransom for all" (I Timothy 2:6); ". . . that he by the grace of God should taste death for every man" (Hebrews 2:9).

It is your inherent right to choose which is at the very heart of the mystery, both of the mystery of *godliness* and of the mystery of *iniquity,* for as we began to see in the fourth chapter, it is man's ability to say "yes" to God in a faith-love relationship of total dependence, producing godliness, which gives him alternatively the ability to say "no" to God in independence—to become a soul dominated by the "flesh," and producing iniquity.

The cross involves for all men everywhere a personal decision which cannot be avoided; for God ". . . now commandeth all men everywhere to repent: because he hath appointed a day, in the which he will judge the world in righteousness by that man whom he hath ordained; whereof he hath given assurance unto all men, in that he hath raised him from the dead" (Acts 17:30 and 31).

This is the compelling love of Christ; God's command to *all men everywhere* to repent is an invitation to Life! He does not mock men who are sorry for their sin, nor does He command men to repent of their sin who cannot be sorry! "For the love of Christ constraineth us; because we thus judge, that if one died for all, then were all dead" (II Corinthians 5:14)—the fact that the Lord Jesus Christ died for all, is ample corroboration of the fact that "in Adam" all died, spiritually dead, "alienated from the life of God"—lamps that are out! How thrilling and wonderful to know, however, that ". . . as in Adam all died, even so in Christ shall all be made alive" (I Corinthians 15:22)!

You can know the indwelling presence of the risen Lord, resident within your human spirit by His Holy Spirit, from the very moment that you receive Christ as your Redeemer! You are then no longer *waiting* for the resurrection—you are enjoying it!

It is true, of course, that there will be a physical resurrection of the body, for ". . . this perishable nature must clothe itself with the imperishable, and this mortality must clothe itself with immortality" (I Corinthians 15:53, *Weymouth*) but this is only incidental compared with the priceless privilege of sharing *now* the very Life of the Lord Jesus Christ Himself!

Consider further with me, however, this important passage in II Corinthians 5:15, "And He died for all, so that all those who live might no longer live to and for themselves, but to and for Him who died and was raised again for their sake." When the apostle refers to "all who live," he is speaking of those who have already been raised from the dead spiritually; they are no longer "in Adam"—dead; they are "in Christ"—alive! He goes on to explain to what end God has raised them to life again. It is that they may no longer live "to and for themselves," but "to and for Him who died and was raised again for their sake"!

In other words, there is to be a remarkable change of attitude and outlook; for Christ died and rose again from the dead to introduce an entirely new principle of human behavior!

To live "to and for yourself" is to "walk after the flesh"!

To live "to and for Christ" is to "walk after the Spirit"!

These are the two principles of human behavior. It is not just a matter of *degree,* it is a matter of *kind;* to be dominated by the "flesh" is to be dominated by the devil; and to be dominated by the Spirit is to be dominated by God.

Two men doing identically the same thing may at the same time, by their identical act, be demonstrating two different principles of behavior which are diametrically opposed to each other.

Both Cain and Abel brought an offering to the Lord (Genesis 4:3-8); and to the undiscerning, it would appear that both were engaged in a sincere act of worship; yet Cain and his offering were both rejected, and God had no respect to them.

Was it the *act* which God rejected, and which made Cain unacceptable? No—it was the principle which governed the act! A principle which made the otherwise innocent act as sinful as the principle which prompted it! He was still living "to and for himself"!

Sin was still lying at the door—the flesh was still dominant; Cain was still convinced of his own superior judgment as to what was good for him, and for that matter, as to what was good for God! He "brought of the fruit of the ground an offering unto the Lord" (Genesis 4:3)—the ground that God had cursed! (Genesis 3:17). Cain "was of that wicked one (*the devil*), and slew his brother. And wherefore slew he him? Because . . ." *in the very act of "worship"* "his own works were evil, and his brother's righteous" (I John 3:12).

To bring an offering to the Lord was for Cain just another way of letting "that wicked one" give expression to his undying hatred of God, and to his unremitting hostility to the Son, for the offering that he brought was in deliberate defiance of the spiritual significance of the lamb that Abel offered. An "act of worship" ended up in an act of cold-blooded murder, but though there may have been some difference in degree between the acts, there was absolutely no difference in kind; it was the devil himself and no other who as we have already seen "was a murderer from the beginning" (John 8:44), who inspired both the "act of worship" and the act of killing Abel; there was death in his religion! When God called his bluff, he was furious and exposed himself for the devil's dupe he was!

It would not really matter whether as a professor in a theological seminary you denied the virgin birth of

Christ, as a pastor from the pulpit you discredited the atoning efficacy of the blood. He shed, or as a church member you participated in those apostate forms of Christless "Christianity" which repudiate His deity and His sinlessness, or drove the nails into His hands and feet upon the cross—all would be equally satisfying to the devil!

Abel on the other hand, through faith ". . . offered to God a more acceptable sacrifice than Cain, and through this faith he had witness borne to him that he was righteous, God bearing witness by accepting his gifts" (Hebrews 11:4, *Weymouth*). It was certainly not the monetary value of the lamb which made either Abel or his gift acceptable, for this may well have been far less than the value of the offering which Cain had brought.

Wherein, then, lay his acceptability?

It was in the principle which governed his act, a principle which demanded total obedience *to* God out of an attitude of total dependence *on* God.

By faith Abel appropriated the spiritual significance of the little lamb, as the symbol of the Lamb of God that taketh away the sin of the world. In humble anticipation he sheltered beneath the "faith-shadow" of a future cross upon which the Prince of Peace would die to kill death dead, and bring him, Abel, back to life again! "And the Lord had respect unto Abel and to his offering" (Genesis 4:4).

What is the principle that governs *your* behavior?

I am not asking you the *nature* of your behavior, I am asking you the *principle* from which it springs!

You will remember that we have seen sin defined in the Bible as independence: "whatsoever is not of faith is sin" (Romans 14:23), an attitude of "lawlessness" (I John 3:4); what then does repentance involve? It involves stepping out of *independence* back into *dependence*—and the measure of your *repentance* will be the measure of your *dependence!*

Every area of your life in which you have not

132

learned to be dependent, is an area of your life in which you have not as yet repented.

Perhaps you are a business-man, and you imagine that once you have crossed the threshold of your office— you are the Boss! Everything you say, goes! This is your little kingdom—perhaps even a mighty empire— but you congratulate yourself upon the fact that you have just what it takes to outbid your competitor, or to out-smart your opponents; you need Christ for your Sunday school class, and you need Christ for some of the other church responsibilities which you shoulder, but right there in the city amidst the stern demands of modern commerce, you are out on your own! It is sink or swim by the might of your own right arm.

Sir! That is just the area in your life where you have *not yet repented!*

Maybe you are a mother, and if there is one thing for which you consider yourself to be completely ade- quate, it is for the business of rearing a family! What you have not learned about child psychology is hardly worth knowing, and the discipline of a well planned family life leaves you little opportunity to get upon your knees. Bath-water and baby-powder have stronger claims upon your time than prayer, and pride of house takes precedence over humility of heart!

Madam! This is just the area of your life in which you have *not yet repented!*

The words flow like water running down a mountain stream when you stand up in the pulpit and intoxicate your congregation with your latest verbal masterpiece; the logic is supreme, and the anecdotes are apt, whilst a dignified deportment gives added point to weighty ut- terances already underlined by gentle gestures with the hands! Aunt Agatha was right when she said that you would one day be a preacher—but she did not know how *fine* a preacher you would be! You have all that it takes to build a thriving church!

Preacher! The pulpit is the place! The place where you have *not yet repented!*

Is it your beautiful voice? . . . or your musical talent? Is it your athletic skill or your academic gift? In what part of your life are you adequate *without* Christ—where to lose *Him* would be to lose *nothing?* That is it! Right there!

That is the place in your life where you have *not yet repented!*

You have been "made alive" in Christ to be exclusively at His disposal, so that by the Holy Spirit He may monopolize your total personality, and give expression to Himself through you in your behavior.

This is what it means to be "filled with the Spirit" (Ephesians 5:18), or to be "godly," as represented by Figure E in the diagram. The Capital "I" is on the cross, and as indicated by the yellow margin at the circumference of circle E, all that you *do* is what Christ *does*, and creates in you the image of all that Christ *is!* "I have been crucified with Christ, and it is no longer I that live, but Christ lives in me; and the life which I now live in the body I live by faith in the Son of God who loved me and gave Himself up for me" (Galatians 2:20, *Weymouth*).

The image will never be perfect or complete down here on earth, but the degree in which by your free consent, you live to and for Christ, is the degree of your spirituality; the degree in which you still live to and for yourself is the degree of your carnality—and the degree in which you have not as yet repented!

It may be, however, that up till now your experience as a Christian has been one of consistent defeat; you are baffled and bewildered at your own impotence, and almost in despair of any possibility of improvement. Sometimes you cry from your heart:

I find therefore this rule, that when I desire to do what is right, evil is there with me. In my inmost self all my sympathy is with the Law of God; but I discover in my faculties a different law, at war with the law of my understanding, and leading me captive to the law which is in my faculties —the law of sin. Unhappy man that I am! who will rescue me from this body of death? (Romans 7:22-24, *Weymouth*).

There is war in your soul, and you will always be baffled and perplexed until you recognize what I have constantly reiterated, that within the soul of every regenerate person there are two powerful forces at work; the constant down-drag of the old, Adamic nature, and the mighty liberating power of Christ the Lord. "So then I myself serve with my understanding the Law of God, but with my lower nature the law of sin" (Romans 7:25, *Weymouth*).

There are two "appetites" at work within you—one insatiably hungry for all that is evil, and hostile to God—and the other insatiably hungry for all that is pure and noble, wholesome and true; the one has its origin in the devil, the other in God.

To be in ignorance of this fact, or to act in defiance of it, will make you as foolish as the Galatian Christians, to whom the Apostle Paul put the following question: "Are you so foolish *and* so senseless *and* so silly? Having begun (your new life Spiritually) with the (Holy) Spirit, are you now reaching perfection [by dependence] on the flesh?" (Galatians 3:3, *Amplified New Testament*).

Having received the very Life of Christ through the Spirit, the only source of Godliness, these foolish Galatians then tried to live the Christian life in the energy of the "flesh," which is only the source of iniquity. They tried to make the leopard change its spots!

Is this what *you* have been doing? Having received *everything* which God can give you *in Christ*, have you been living as though God had given you *nothing*,—as though everything depended on *you*?

It is as though you were born with a battered, old-vintage Ford car in the garage, with broken springs, faulty brakes and dirty plugs—the flesh! Then you are born-again, and there is a brand new Cadillac—the Spirit—alongside the rusty old Ford in the garage—but instead of going out in the brand new Cadillac, you drive around in your old tin crate—honking, snorting, puffing and blowing in a cloud of smoke, "giving your testimony," and telling folk about your lovely new car!

Your testimony would be as flat as your tires! You would spend all your time asking God for spares: "O God, please give me new springs; and please God, give me new plugs!" . . . and God would do nothing of the sort! He would say, "Stick it in the dump! It's only fit for the scrap heap—so bury it! Go out in the brand new Cadillac I have given you—it has power enough and to spare!"—for "It is the Spirit that quickeneth; the flesh profiteth nothing" (John 6:63).

The death of Christ upon the cross accomplished something much more than your redemption from the penalty of sin. It put your *pride* on the scrap-heap and *you* in the dump!

However little we may be able to explain it, "We know that our old (unrenewed) self was nailed to the cross with Him in order that [our] body, [which is the instrument] of sin, might be made ineffective *and* inactive for evil, that we might no longer be the slaves of sin" (Romans 6:6, *Amplified New Testament*).

In other words, as illustrated by the center circle in Figure E (see diagram), there must not only be a Cross on the Hill, but a Cross in your Heart!

The "self" that sin makes of you was taken by the Lord Jesus Christ into death with Him—that you might be delivered not only from sin's penalty, but also from its power. Your soul is released from sin's evil influence, so that you may become the "self" that Christ makes of you—"a new creature: old things are passed away; behold, all things are become new" (II Corinthians 5:17).

The Capital "I" has been crucified with Christ so

136

that God may "have right of way" into every area of your personality, at liberty to reproduce Himself once more in you, and transform you into His own likeness— and that is *godliness!*

We were buried therefore with Him by the baptism into death, so that just as Christ was raised from the dead by the glorious [power] of the Father, so we too might habitually live *and* behave in newness of life. For if we have become one with Him by sharing a death like His, we shall also be [one with Him in sharing] His resurrection [by a new life lived for God] (Romans 6:4 and 5, *Amplified New Testament*).

However, just as the death of Christ *for* you is only *potential* until by a deliberate and voluntary *act* of faith you appropriate its efficacy for your redemption, so *your* death *with* Christ is only potential unless by a deliberate and voluntary *attitude* of faith you appropriate its efficacy for your sanctification—enabling God to put you once more to that intelligent use for which He created you, and for which Christ has now redeemed you.

For by the death He died He died to sin [ending His relation to it] once for all, and the life that He lives He is living to God—in unbroken fellowship with Him. Even so consider yourselves also dead to sin *and* your relation to it broken, but [that you are] alive to God—living in unbroken fellowship with Him—in Christ Jesus (Romans 6:10 and 11, *Amplified New Testament*).

You are to live exclusively "to and for Christ," and to consider yourself "alive to God" only by virtue of what you are "in Him."

You cannot *accomplish* your own redemption, and you cannot *accomplish* your own sanctification! It is "According as his divine power hath given unto us all things that pertain unto life and godliness, through the knowledge of him that hath called us to glory and

137

virtue" (II Peter 1:3): *faith takes* what *God gives,* and *God gives* what *man needs! All* that he needs!

All that God *gives,* which is all that you *need,* He gives to you in Christ, "That no flesh should glory in his presence. But of him are ye in Christ Jesus, who of God is made unto us wisdom, and righteousness, and sanctification, and redemption" (I Corinthians 1:29 and 30).

The degree to which by a deliberate, voluntary attitude of faith you are reckoning yourself to be dead "with Christ" to all that you are "in Adam" and *alive* to God in all that you are "in Christ"—is the degree to which the redemptive purpose of God has been wrought out in your life—and this is the only valid estimate of your worth! Everything else is a *dead loss!* "Consequently, from now on we estimate *and* regard no one from a [purely] human point of view—in terms of natural standards of value" (II Corinthians 5:16, *Amplified New Testament*).

Pointing to an affluent looking gentleman coming into the church, I might say to you (if I were mischievous enough), "How much is he worth?" and maybe you would reply, "If he's worth a dollar, he's worth a million!" . . . and I would say to you, "I did not ask *how much money he had in the bank!* I simply asked you how much he was *worth!*"

A man could have all the money in all the banks in all the world, and be worth *nothing*—so far as God is concerned, if he were still living "to and for himself"! The measure of a man's worth is the measure in which he no longer lives "to and for himself," but "to and for Jesus Christ." *No more and no less!*

How much are *you* worth?

You tell me that you have just completed your church building program, and that the Board has just appointed a new minister; that's fine, but pardon me for asking—how much is he worth? "Why," you say, "he has a most distinguished academic record," and you

138

begin to enlarge upon the letters after his name, but you will forgive me if I interrupt, I am sure. It is excellent that a man should take the trouble to be highly qualified, but I did not ask you *how clever he was at mastering facts, or in passing examinations,* I simply asked how much he was *worth!*

A man's worth is not primarily a matter of *scholarship,* it is essentially a matter of *relationship*— relationship to Jesus Christ. It is, of course, perfectly possible and perfectly legitimate to have both, and this is to be commended—but we should always remind ourselves that—

> . . . the foolishness of God is wiser than men, and the weakness of God is stronger than men.
> For consider, brethren, your own calling. Not many worldlywise, not many influential, not many of noble birth have been called. But God has chosen the foolish things of the world in order to shame its wise men; and God has chosen the weak things of the world in order to shame what is strong; and the mean and despised things of the world— things that are nothing—God has chosen in order to bring to nothing things that are; to prevent any mortal man from boasting before God (I Corinthians 1:25-29, *Weymouth*).

How much are *you* worth?

There was a time when Paul the Apostle, as Saul of Tarsus, hated Christ and persecuted the Church, and he had done so because he had still regarded Christ from a purely human point of view—in terms of natural standards of value.

Had these "natural standards of value" been spiritually valid, Saul of Tarsus would have been right, and Paul the Apostle would have been wrong!

To Saul, according to all the facts as he knew them, and as they were commonly accepted by all the "people that mattered," Jesus Christ was the illegitimate child of an unfaithful woman, so that by all normally accepted standards of society, He was an outcast! Socially, how much was He worth? Nothing!

Born of peasant stock, His schooling was negligible, sufficing only to equip Him for the humble duties of a common craftsman. Professionally, how much was He worth? Nothing!

A fanatical street-preacher and a rabble rouser, He was totally repudiated by all the ecclesiastical dignitaries of His day, and having had absolutely no theological training whatever, was looked upon with supreme contempt by all that called itself scholarship amongst those who searched the Scriptures. Ecclesiastically, theologically and intellectually how much was He worth? Nothing!

His financial standing was such that He even had to borrow a coin for one of His far-fetched illustrations! He was an incorrigible "scrounger" by all "natural standards of value," for He had no home of His own. Born in a borrowed stable, He lived and dined in borrowed homes; He rode upon a borrowed donkey, was crucified on a borrowed cross and buried in a borrowed tomb! He was bankrupt from the start! Financially, how much was He worth? By all "natural standards of value"—nothing!

Shall we be angry with Saul of Tarsus? Was his judgment insincere? Were the conclusions to which he came not entirely reasonable?

If the Lord Jesus Christ were to appear in the world today under similar circumstances, what congregation would call Him to be their pastor? What university or Bible college or training institute would appoint Him to their faculty? What missionary organization would invite Him on their board, or even send Him to the field? Who would make Him chairman of the building committee?

Maybe our standards of value are as wrong today as were those of Saul in his day!

Something happened, however, which changed Saul of Tarsus completely, the old standards of value went by the board, and everything assumed an entirely new perspective!

The *values themselves* had not changed! It was simply that in a dazzling encounter on the road to Damascus, Saul of Tarsus saw "the glory of God in the face of Jesus Christ"! (II Corinthians 4:6). He looked into the face of a *Man* and saw *God* and was blinded by the sight,—for he saw ". . . the perfect imprint *and* very image of [God's] nature" (Hebrews 1:3, *Amplified New Testament*).

In one blinding, crushing moment of humiliation his own utter worthlessness was exposed to the stubborn heart of this proud enemy of the faith! "Circumcised the eighth day, of the stock of Israel, of the tribe of Benjamin, an Hebrew of the Hebrews; as touching the law, a Pharisee; concerning zeal, persecuting the church; touching the righteousness which is in the law, blameless" (Philippians 3:5 and 6), by all "natural standards of value" this man was worth *everything*—and had already outstripped many of his Jewish contemporaries in his boundless devotion to the traditions of his ancestors (Galatians 1:14, *New English Bible*), but in the light of this new discovery of God, he could only say:

> But all such assets I have written off because of Christ. I would say more: I count everything sheer loss, because all is far outweighed by the gain of knowing Christ Jesus my Lord, for whose sake I did in fact lose everything. I count it so much garbage, for the sake of gaining Christ and finding myself incorporate in him, with no righteousness of my own, no legal rectitude, but the righteousness which comes from faith in Christ, given by God in response to faith (Philippians 3:7-9, *New English Bible*).

Saul of Tarsus suddenly discovered that a man is worth only as much *as can be seen of God in him;* and that he was in the presence of the Man in whom (to use his own description) ". . . the whole fulness of Deity

141

(the God-head), continues to dwell in bodily form—giving complete expression of the divine nature" (Colossians 2:9, *Amplified New Testament*), and that this *Man* was *Jesus Christ* whom he was persecuting!

From that moment on, nothing else mattered! Saul of Tarsus stopped being Saul of Tarsus, and became Paul the Apostle! He was *out* of Adam, and he was *in* Christ, and the "law of the Spirit of Life" began to operate, introducing the new principle of human behavior which made him a "new creature"!

Paul had found reality in God, and the "show" was over! He could afford to discard his "make-up," and lay aside the musty costumes of a religious performance! The pompous self-esteem of a godless society no longer impressed him, nor the honors it could bestow upon its servile devotees!

The Apostle was emancipated! He was released from the hollow art of living in a fool's paradise of faulty values; a world of artificial standards anchored to a cloud, and blown by every wind of fashion!—"God forbid," he says, "that I should glory, save in the cross of our Lord Jesus Christ, by whom the world is crucified unto me, and I unto the world" (Galatians 6:14)!

Losing his life—he found it! Dying to self and buried with Christ he found himself alive again—*in God;* for in that blinding flash of glory on the Damascus Road, the whole *Mystery of Godliness* had become an *open secret* in the face of Jesus Christ!

He had discovered how much he was worth—*nothing!*

To discover that, is to discover how much Christ is worth—*everything!*

When you are willing to *obey* what you have *discovered*, and let the Truth *behave*, then the Lord Jesus Christ will fill what you are—NOTHING, with what He is—EVERYTHING, and that indeed will be SOMETHING!

With the wrong man out, and the Right Man in, how

wealthy God will have made you! Good friend, before you lay this book aside embrace by faith these great and precious promises, and commit yourself to Christ for all that which He is committed to in you; He waits to fill you with Himself and share with you the Secret of the Mystery! "Even the mystery which hath been hid from ages and from generations, but now is made manifest to his saints. To whom God would make known what is the riches of the glory of this mystery among the Gentiles; which is *Christ in you,* the hope of glory" (Colossians 1:26 and 27, italics for emphasis).